Baby Roulette

a humorous and revealing insight into the world of IVF

by

Rachel Watson

authorHOUSE™

1663 LIBERTY DRIVE, SUITE 200
BLOOMINGTON, INDIANA 47403
(800) 839-8640
WWW.AUTHORHOUSE.COM

First published by AuthorHouse 12/13/05

ISBN: 1-4208-8155-8 (sc)

Printed in the United States of America
Bloomington, Indiana

This book is printed on acid-free paper.

A donation from the proceeds of the sale of this book will go to Infertility Network UK.

Infertility Network UK is a national charity set up to provide information, advice, and support to anyone suffering from infertility through a network of local support groups, advice line, website, factsheets, and quarterly magazine. Contact us on 08701 188088 or visit our website at www. infertilitynetworkuk.com.

For my loving husband,
who made all this possible.

Chapter 1
Red Meanie Monsters

Bella had just finished skimming her way through her daily commuter newspaper only to engage herself in another 'How Does She Manage To Do It?' piece of journalistic fodder. Predictably, there was a photo of a mid-thirties woman in a city suit with a blonde manicured 'I'm in control' look. The second photo showed the woman at home, slightly more tousled and barefoot cooking fairy cakes under the adoring gaze of her husband and beautiful children.

As the train clinked along Bella imagined an article featuring herself as the centrepiece, 'How Does She Manage Not To Do It?'

Bella would take centre stage looking hormonal and bloated with an air of desperation. Maybe the photographer could add a few IVF syringes to replace the fairy cakes, a desperate looking husband and maybe a woeful baby-replacement cat to complete the happy picture.

The train ground to a halt and Bella tossed the paper to the floor leaving the happy, smiling family crumpled on the ground.

Bella dashed to Starbucks for a pre-menstrual comforter hot chocolate and peach muffin combo. Clutching her comforters Bella headed to the office with a planned en-route have-I-failed-to-conceive-again knicker check in the train station loo before facing the daily onslaught at work.

Bella had been stuck in the same job for eleven years, managing travel for colourful characters within a music company. Everyone around Bella thought her job was glamorous and exciting. If you call being available 24/7 for a group of highly-strung assistants barking orders at you to deliver the impossible then I guess it was.

The artists were just names booked on planes and hotels. Bella never met them nor even spoke to them.

Bella downloaded an email from the assistant to the latest signing demanding an explanation as to why her artiste had not been seated in 1A from London to Paris. Bella could never work out if the travel bookers had selective deafness or amnesia. She had gone to great lengths to explain at the time of the booking that the seat had already been taken probably by someone more important or a regular punter with a silver smurf badge or whatever the latest executive card scheme was. Diplomatically, Bella left out the bit about someone potentially being more important and the smurf badge.

After eleven years of seat 1A tantrums Bella had learned to be gracious in the face of abuse and fired off a standard thank-you-for-your-feedback email complete with the appropriate grovel paragraph inserted from her sizeable collection.

In Bella's draft folder she had completed a range of truthful replies mostly addressed 'Dear Assistant From Hell', on the basis that Bella would be fired for pressing 'Send'. These remained stored in draft for perusal on day one of period days. In fact most of the draft emails were written on day one of period days.

Bella was burned out by the demands of the assistants from hell and their darling artists, despite having grand dreams of finding another job and sending all of her draft emails on the last day, Bella remained a loyal and compliant employee. Deep down Bella couldn't face going to the market and trying to sell herself to a new employer. After two years of trying to conceive their much longed for child, anything else that required energy and focus seemed impossible other than on New Year's Eve after copious amounts of gin and champagne.

Bella suddenly snapped into action when her phone started trilling, cue, "you are a useless bloody travel agent, I could do better on the Internet, I cannot believe your voicemail telling me Alicia's favourite hotel suite is full in L.A."

Bella grabbed her stress ball, a smart purchase by husband Alex, and made soundless thumps with it against the desk. Just at the point when the assistant screeched the obligatory "So what are you going to do about it?" Bella's period cramps started. Bella's overriding need to get rid of this woman and visit the loo to confirm her latest failed conception attempt prompted her instant ability to bullshit.

"I have arranged a superior suite at the Beverley Hills Hotel for the same price," at the same time Bella flicked through the latest celeb magazine and randomly picked a hot USA starlet and added the pièce de résistance, "Holly B just stayed in the same suite and the celeb pack has already moved on from the property you previously selected."

Cue the assistant from heaven, "Darling you are a total star and always are." Bella switched off the parting platitudes and kissing sounds as she scrambled for some organic tampons to stuff down her skirt to take to the loo.

Bella couldn't decide which would be less stressful - checking her knickers for confirmation of failing to get pregnant again or composing another apology email to placate the last assistant when she discovers that one previously mentioned starlet has never stayed at the alternative hotel and the hottest celeb pack are all at the other one, that's why it's full. Writing responses to complaints before she had received them; bloody hell not even her highly-strung boss could accuse her of not being proactive.

Bella's phone beeped with a text message. Which bloody idiot wanted to harass her next? Bella saw the message was from Alex and read on. It was the normal tentative enquiry about her failure to conceive again hidden under a veil of innocence, 'have the red meanie monsters arrived?' he tactfully enquired.

Bella sloped off to the loo, validated the invasion of the monsters and texted a message back confirming the invasion. An instant 'I love you' message beeped back at her.

In truth Alex's innocent sounding text message translated to 'do I really have to do a sperm test or have we hit the jackpot?' For two years Alex had managed to convince her it was only a matter of time. He was right, it was only a matter of time before she dragged him to the doctors or packed his bloody bags.

Bella and Alex's eight year marriage had managed to survive Bella's screaming clients ringing at all hours of the day and an average of four "sorry I'm late and there's nothing in the fridge" nights a week. A takeaway kebab with an industrial strength gin and tonic normally repaired any potential rift.

Bella looked at the simple 'I love you' message on her phone again. Would he still love her? What if they went through all the dreaded fertility tests and the net result was that Bella was the one guilty as charged of being unable to provide her loving husband with the child they had been dreaming of for the last eight years and trying to conceive for the last two?

An ominous email pinged up on Bella's screen entitled 'Totally Unacceptable'. Apparently the pre-ordered triangular buckwheat pillow had not been available as requested during the stay in New York arranged for one of their more established artists (i.e. washed up old has been). The subsequent lack of sleep induced by the absence of the pre-ordered buckwheat-pillow meant she couldn't give the public what they wanted at the launch of her third greatest hits album, hence only 30 people had bothered to ask for signed copies.

Bella wondered if the hotel had access to her ailing record sales and had shipped all the buckwheat out to more successful artists they were likely to see again.

Totally Unacceptable. The fact she and Alex couldn't manage to conceive this month on their second year of infertility anniversary, *that* was totally unacceptable, not the fact that some miserable old has been could not get her precious bloody pillow. Bella was really starting to lose the will.

Bella phoned Alex. As usual, he didn't pick up, so she left one of her slightly less controlled time of the month messages "Alex, I've had enough of this, it is totally unacceptable (her phrase of the day), whether you like it or not we are going to the bloody doctors and if it means you doing one in a cupboard over a copy of Razzle so be it. I cannot take any more of this crap. Love you, honey bunny."

After receiving the standard icy response from the gatekeeper receptionist at the doctors, Bella managed to secure an appointment for the following week. The initial timeframes had been shortened on the production of some hysterical day one sobbing. Bella hadn't bothered to check Alex's diary – tough, she was sick of his "it will happen one day or if it's meant to be" crap. Meant to be, meant to be? Wasn't that a rather paradoxical statement? Meant to be what? Childless and miserable?

Bella submerged herself in her work for the rest of the day and made a conscious decision to leave work at a reasonable time to accommodate a large gin and tonic, which she hoped would take the edge off the conversation she planned to have with Alex.

Bella watched a couple of yummy mummys meet their fraught looking husbands at the train station complete with their highly charged children thrilled to be seeing Daddy. Make that a pint of gin and tonic.

Said gin and tonic was poured and devoured, Bella realised she still had her raincoat on. The look would be completed by the addition of a park bench and a bottle of meths she mused.

Bella heard the key in the door and immediately regretted the second gin and tonic to calm her nerves and the third to stop her hysterical sobbing.

Alex walked into the kitchen and started mumbling on about a concert he had seen in the Evening Standard whilst busily checking the calendar in the kitchen. Suddenly Bella saw Alex's shoulders tense as he registered the 'Bella, Alex - Doctors Appointment' scrawled in red with big stars around it.

"What's this?"

Bella gulped down some more G&T.

"Didn't you listen to my message Alex?"

"What message?"

"The one I left on your mobile six hours ago."

"Bella, there is no message on my mobile."

Oh no, not again – Bella started to feel sick, very sick. Her boss Anthony was the next speed dial number on her mobile; bloody hell she'd done it again.

"Alex, we need to see a Doctor, I can't stand this every month. Clearly something is wrong, it doesn't take two years to still *not* have a baby."

Alex pulled his coat off and launched straight into his standard response. "We've been through this, let's just keep trying – it will happen, you just need to remain positive."

"Remain positive? Is it my fault we can't get pregnant because I am not positive? Alex what are you afraid of?"

"I'm not afraid. I just want us to give it a bit longer."

Bella slammed down her drink. Alex had finally pushed her to the limit.

"Alex, after two years of trying, I have tried to be positive. I have swallowed every herbal concoction known to mankind, stood on my head after sex, bought a bloody kitten with behavioural problems to try and develop my maternal instinct. I have even shoved crystals down my bra and you tell me to give it a bit sodding longer."

Alex started opening a bottle of wine.

"We *are* going to this appointment Alex."

Alex trudged off and returned with his latest handheld electronic diary gadget and snapped, "It's in my diary."

Bella ate a bag of crisps for dinner and went to bed, hiding a 'Coping With Infertility' guide under a copy of 'OK'. She sobbed again at the well-thumbed case study of a couple dealing with their test results.

Chapter 2
Confidentiality Clause

Bella flicked through her emails. Damn it, there was one from her boss, Anthony, asking her to call him urgently. The email had been sent at 0201. Bella only received middle of the night emails from Anthony when he had something on his mind such as a client having screamed at him and he did not know what to do, or a strange voicemail from an employee....

Considering the highlights of her rather disturbing voicemail included direct references to Razzle and pregnancy, no doubt he was already calculating her maternity leave dates, hence the moonlit sweat.

Reluctantly Bella dialled Anthony's number and braced herself. Anthony had been blessed with many diva-like qualities with the exception of any definable talent. In a past life he had been an agent to a number of vaguely recognisable names and after his business failed to generate any notable income he sought employment and became Bella's boss. Anthony could be extremely amusing with his overdramatic responses to business as usual but a bloody pain in the arse when Bella was up to her eyes in the daily grind of seat 1A dramas. At the age of fifty he was struggling to relate to some of their clients whose drug fuelled demands even Bella struggled to make sense of and he constantly fretted that he would lose his job. Anthony had supported his partner Clive for over 10 years, Clive the alleged writer, although the only writing Bella had ever seen Clive produce was on Anthony's cheque book.

"Bella, darling how are you?"

"Just fine Anthony and how are you?"

"Fabbie sweetie, fabbie – now we have to do a little presentation to a prospective client, you know this new hip and happening little company our darling customer has just acquired. Really high profile and they think the demands of their artists are above anything planet earth has experienced before. Bottom line is I need you there, sweetie, to, you know, sell the story, walk the talk, show them how invincible you are in the face of adversity, give them examples of how we get rooms in hotels that are full, show them how easy it is to get their artists what they want when they want it and totally make it real."

"When is it Anthony?"

"Next Wednesday darling."

Bella's heart sank, it was D Day as in day of the doctors, after Alex had finally entered the appointment into his raspberry or whatever his latest hand held device was called. She was not cancelling.

"Sorry, I can't make Wednesday."

Bella immediately moved the phone two inches further away from her ear. Anthony launched his first missile of the day.

"Bella I don't do the word can't."

Was that a double negative? Bella wondered.

"I have a Doctor's appointment that I really can't change."

"A bloody Doctor's appointment," raged Anthony "is it life or death?"

Considering the circumstances, this was quite a poignant statement. Bella didn't want to allude to the fact it was a situation relating to a new life or lack of it so she decided to not respond directly to the question.

"Er.... It's just really important that I go to the doctors on that day," mumbled Bella.

"Oh God, you're not sodding pregnant are you, because I am just losing the will to live right now."

This at least was one line of enquiry Bella could respond positively to. "No I am definitely not pregnant."

"Oh good, that's a relief."

After several minutes of Anthony's feel sorry for me act Bella felt sorry for him and agreed to attend the meeting. It would mean that she had one hour to get from the meeting to the doctors. It was a fair compromise if it meant a tantrum free week with Anthony.

Bella spent the rest of the week preparing a presentation for Anthony, retaining the usual death-by-PowerPoint format.

Since the confrontation with Alex regarding the impending Doctor's visit, Bella noticed that he had become withdrawn. Other than the gin fuelled screaming match they had not really talked about the visit or any potential outcome.

Bella decided to arrange a dinner with Alex the night before they were due to visit the doctors. Hopefully by the end of their first bottle of wine she could gauge how Alex would react to the outcome of any tests. If she was the cause of the lack of offspring could he continue to love her, the woman who couldn't give him the child they both desired?

What if it was Alex's, you know, sperm swimming in the wrong direction or not swimming at all? I mean what do you say when the guilty party is revealed? "Oh darling I love you anyway irrespective of the fact we can't have children. P.S. are sperm banks available online?"

Bella tried to calm down and think of the benefits of knowing why it wasn't happening. Maybe knowing means you can find a solution or eventually move on, so every month isn't filled with trepidation and failed dreams.

Bella knew they needed to discuss this and doubled her efforts to finish Anthony's presentation so she could make sure they could have dinner tomorrow night.

Alex looked at the bottom of his empty beer glass and joined the queue at the bar with the hope of securing and finishing his third beer in peace before Guy arrived. Alex had arranged to see Guy on the basis that he was his oldest friend and he needed to talk sperm tests. Up until now Bella and Alex remained united in their silence regarding their inability to conceive. Alex was sure that Bella had confided with a couple of her inner circle, but generally quips about the pattering of little feet were deferred with references to their careers and the pattering of their dysfunctional kitten's paws.

Careers - that was a bloody joke. Alex always thought Bella was stuck in a thankless job and whilst the income was dependable it was low. As for Alex he didn't know if he would stay in his job from one day to the next. He had started in the City when the market was booming and made easy money. Now he was stuck on a trading desk at a bank in a wing-it role that could end at any time and on top of all of this Bella was hell bent on having a baby.

Their lack of ability to conceive suited Alex. Of course he wanted a child as much as Bella did but he didn't see the rush. On a weekly basis Bella would read articles about diminishing egg reserves and people in their late thirties resorting to IVF. Life with Bella was like living with a bloody egg timer and he felt he was watching every grain of sand pass through.

The most difficult part for Alex was seeing Bella so unhappy, despite the mood swings and the fact that one week out of every four was hell, he knew that he still loved her deeply. When Alex first met Bella on a drunken night out in the City he knew straight away he wanted to marry her. Alex's past relationships had lasted on average six months but when he met Bella, fresh faced and devoid of any baggage and ten years younger, he decided she was the one.

Their first years of marriage had been blissful, plenty of free travel with Bella's job, endless drunken dinner parties and a general carefree approach to life. Alex's job was going very well and when Bella, on one dusky evening in Bali, suggested she stop taking the pill, Alex ran back to the room with her and flushed the pills down the loo and joined her in bed with the complimentary hotel fizz.

In fact the first 12 months of trying for a baby had been quite enjoyable from Alex's perspective. Bella initiated sex most of the time and it still felt like a spontaneous act. Once the first year had passed and multiple dirty weekends away had not produced an offspring, the tempo changed and Bella's collection of pregnancy books were gradually replaced with books on infertility and the cupboards became full of foul smelling tea and herbs.

Every morning Bella would curse that her temperature graph didn't look like the one in the book. Alex had to agree it had more dips than the Footsie 100 share index. He read in a book that the odds on young fertile couples conceiving when they first start are only 33%. For most couples the average is lower, on average one in five or six chance on every cycle, about the same as trying to throw a six with a dice, so Alex reckoned it could take a while.

So they drifted on, Alex becoming increasingly bored with the subject and Bella becoming increasingly obsessed. Sex had become routine, shag to schedule, and if you could ignore Bella doing post-coital headstands, supposedly to help the sperm reach the egg, this whole baby-making thing was starting to lose its appeal.

One of the worst things was Bella's obsession with pregnancy tests. The market research people at Tesco must have been baffled as once a month the Tesco van would pull up complete with Tampons and pregnancy tests. Alex was sure that at the rate Bella went through the tests the main market for the product was for those who couldn't get pregnant, not those who could. Bella's main excuse for testing every month was so she could stop drinking alcohol if she knew she was pregnant. Normally less than a day after the test, Bella would either stomp to the airing cupboard to fetch her tampax or leave a slightly deranged voicemail to the effect that it was period time. God, those times of the month were bad. Alex had even started to text Bella to find out if her period had arrived so he could prepare himself with an extra beer or six at the station in advance of his depressing homecoming. Of course Alex was always disappointed but it didn't tip him into a sequence of hysterical sobbing, yoga poses and lying down with bits of coloured rock called crystals or something. Alex thought that the problem was probably compounded by these strange rocks. After all, Kryptonite had drained Superman of his powers. This stuff was probably affecting his sperm count through the ether.

Bella had called Alex earlier to inform him she had booked dinner at their favourite eating-place. Alex had read into this that he was about to receive his pre-doctors sermon i.e. thou shalt not make jokes regarding sperm cupboards, thou shalt not irrevocably lie about alcohol consumption and lifestyle and thou shalt not say we are not in any hurry to conceive. This is why he had called Guy earlier, even though Guy knew bugger all about sperm tests. Guy was still pissed off with the fact that he and his wife had managed to conceive their third whilst breast feeding their second and blamed his inability to sink more than five pints on chronic sleep deprivation. Alex just wanted a male's perspective on how to deal with the whole Bella egg timer thing.

Alex saw Guy push his way through a group of city types lusting after the secretarial intake and make his way towards Alex. Guy looked awful. His hair needed a good cut and his suit looked like it could walk to the dry cleaners.

"Can't tell you how glad I was to receive your call mate. Jen can't stop throwing up and number two is teething, it's like a bloody battleground at home. I told Jen you needed to see me urgently, sounded like you were having a major life crisis, couldn't really hear her response as her mouth was full of sick but she knows I'm out for most of the night. Beer?"

Alex smiled and nodded, Guy lived his life in permanent chaos but always seemed to get by. After about ten minutes Guy returned with four pints of beer.

"Thought we could save the queue next time. I tell you what a bloody day I've had, this jumped up little prat the agency has just employed has slated my latest client pitch to Tabitha. So I get dragged into the witches' lair for a post-mortem on my work. Her senior contact at the client has given her the heads up that they think our campaigns are lacking originality. No doubt she only solicited the feedback after the jumped up prat who is after my job went into overdrive on her flip charts earlier. Anyway I bloody told her straight, I know the client and I'll deliver the right pitch, whilst the witch spent the whole time staring at the baby sick on my suit. Why the hell did I go into advertising, anyway, what's your crisis?"

"I've got to get my ding-a-ling out at the doctors."

Guy spat out some of his beer.

"Bloody hell mate, who did you catch that from, I mean, Bella hasn't been sleeping around has she?"

Alex couldn't help but laugh. "No, I haven't caught anything, that's the whole point mate. I've been trying to get Bella pregnant for the last two years and nothing has happened on the old baby producing front."

"So is your sperm, like, not working? Wish I had the same problem at times, especially when the little sods are screaming at night."

"No we don't know what the problem is. I have to go to the doctors this week with Bella and then we start all the tests."

"So it could be Bella, she could be like sterile or barren or whatever they call it?"

"We just don't know mate, the thing is this whole thing is seriously tipping Bella over the edge, it's like living with an egg timer as she's becoming increasingly desperate for kids. I want to wait a bit longer you know with all the crap going on in my job, but she's determined to drag me down to the doctors for a good old prodding."

"Bloody hell mate, I don't know what to say. Jen seems to be born to breed and I've had no problems in the old sperm department. I guess there's no point in delaying the inevitable, I mean if there was something wrong with my sperm I'd want to know. Has Bella talked to Jen about this?"

"No idea."

Alex guessed Bella hadn't, whilst Jen was in the inner circle he doubted Bella would discuss their conception problems with the leader of an ever increasing brood.

Alex and Guy downed several more pints and discussed how rubbish work was before staggering off towards the station. It was well past Guy's curfew. Alex didn't have one tonight as it wasn't a shag-to-schedule night and Bella was happy to have a quiet night in with a few glasses of wine and some foul smelling nail varnish.

Just as they were stumbling onto the train, Guy's mobile started ringing. He showed Alex the caller id 'Dragon'. Alex assumed it was Jen and picked up a battered copy of the Evening Standard from a nearby seat.

"For God's sake Jen, I'll be back in 45 minutes. Look, I'll read her a story. No, I don't smell of beer and fags. Look, I'm not going to apologise. Alex is about to find out if his sperm is swimming in the wrong direction and needs my support."

With that parting shot, Guy hit the red button and fell asleep.

No doubt Jen would grill Guy, and Alex would have to confess to Bella that he had confided in Guy. Damn it, he should have added a confidentiality clause, one that Guy could relate to, like on his stag weekend. What goes on tour stays on tour.

Chapter 3
Domestic Drama

Bella sent Anthony's presentation and his lines at 7:30 a.m. with the faint hope he would call through his numerous re-writes before lunchtime. Bella wanted to leave on time to spend at least an hour getting ready for her dinner with Alex. At least if she was deemed the infertile one she could make the barren look a good one. Looking good or even half decent was something she was struggling to achieve these days without numerous pots and potions.

Bella called Anthony's assistant who tried to find a window for the presentation to be reviewed. Bella muttered something about finding the door if a window wasn't found before 4 p.m. Eventually they agreed that Anthony would review the presentation at 2 p.m. and call her at 3 p.m. Bella decided to go out and buy a new top and lipstick for dinner.

Anthony finally called at 4 p.m. Bella knew any pots and potions time had gone out of the window, sod it.

"Bella darling I've reviewed the deck, just a few changes. Do you think we could change the font and maybe add a few graphs?"

Anthony's complete inability to effectively write a presentation was often highlighted by his desire for different fonts and pictures. He could never critique the content, as he rarely understood it. Two hours later, Anthony finally agreed that the presentation was acceptable. Bella raced home.

Bella managed to grab a shower, re-patch her hair and make up and squeeze into a skirt that she bought before they were married, Bella looked at the clock - 7.30 p.m. and no Alex and guess what his mobile was switched off. Not now thought Bella. Bella knew that Alex went through phases of drinking before he came home.

Normally this was a response to his job going even worse than usual or if Bella was in a day one hormonal haze. They had 30 minutes to get to dinner. This was so typical of their life, always up against the clock. Bella started to feel her anger swell inside her, reaching for the Gin bottle was probably not the best idea as she would probably have to drive. Sod it, she needed a drink. She booked a taxi for 10 minutes before their dinner reservation. The poor bloke from the taxi company was used to arriving at their house when Alex was still in the shower and they needed to be some place in 5 minutes.

Bella was halfway through her second gin and tonic when she heard a cab draw up outside, followed by a second cab. Alex bundled out of the second cab and she saw him swaying as he paid the driver. Bloody hell, he'd been drinking again.

Bella snatched her keys from the side and stormed outside.

"How many have you had?"

"Enough."

Bella knew enough was a code word for 'too much and you are not interrogating me'.

"We better go straight to dinner."

Alex nodded and they jumped in the cab. Sensing the atmosphere the cabbie remained silent.

At the restaurant, Bella ordered wine whilst Alex downed a Diet Coke in a lame attempt to lend some sobriety to the occasion.

"How was your day?" asked Bella.

"Fine."

Bella knew if one-word answers were the order of the evening this was pointless. She pretended to study the menu even though she always ordered the same thing. Bella fought back the tears that were choking the back of her throat.

Alex nearly downed his first glass of wine and instantly became more animated. Bella could not believe he was telling jokes with the waiters.

Bella felt the tears streaming down her face.

"Bloody hell Bella, what's the matter?"

Whatever state Alex was in, he hated to see her upset.

"I just can't do this Alex, I want to go home."

"We've only just got here and besides, we haven't eaten."

"I can't eat Alex. I feel physically sick. I booked this meal so we could talk about tomorrow, not to get pissed and joke with the waiters."

"I've not had any lunch," pleaded Alex.

Honestly, there could be a bloody global disaster involving Alex and he would still forage for food.

"We'll just have a main course and leave then, and stop downing that wine."

"Don't show me up in public Bella. You know how much I hate it when you do that."

"You're doing a pretty good job of that yourself Alex."

Bella forced down her dinner and they were back at home within the hour. Once they were in the confines of their own home Bella started to sob hysterically.

Alex couldn't take this. He hated to see her upset.

"Oh God Bella please don't cry. I'm sorry I ruined dinner. It's just the whole thing with my job and this not getting pregnant stuff. I can't deal with all of it at once."

"So how do you deal with it Alex, find solace in the bottom of a pint glass?"

"What do you do Bella, order another pregnancy test and bottle of gin from Tesco online?"

Bella stormed out of the lounge and ran past their shell-shocked kitten straight into the bathroom where she locked the door and fell to the floor sobbing. Bella felt so desperate. Her life seemed to be just falling apart. She wanted this baby so much but what the hell was going on with Alex? Alex had been like this for the last year. He had been staying out after work, drinking and was starting to look like a bloated whale.

"Bella, come out darling we can sort this out."

Bella reluctantly opened the door and Alex joined her on the floor.

"I love you Bella. I promise I'll be on my best behaviour at the doctors. I'll do my sperm test and frequent as many hospital cupboards as I need to. If getting pregnant is going to make you happy, then let's do all this stuff."

"God, Alex, it's not just about me being happy. I want *us* to be happy. You know I love you but I don't just need you to be on your best behaviour, I need you emotionally and I just don't think you know what that means."

"I will support you. I'm just struggling right now, you know with the stuff at work. I promise I'll try harder."

"What if I'm infertile?"

"What do you mean?"

"You know we go through all the tests and I cannot have children and you in theory could with someone else?"

"Bella, what do you mean have kids with someone else? I married you kids or no kids. I don't want anyone else. If it is not meant to be then we are going to have to deal with that but it's not about who is infertile. It is our problem irrespective of the outcome of the tests. I mean it could easily be either one of us or both but it just doesn't matter, as we're in this together."

"That's all I wanted to hear. Why did you have to go out and get pissed before the dinner."

"I dunno, just thought you were going to lecture me about the doctor's appointment and couldn't handle it."

"Let's go to bed. I have a presentation with Anthony first thing and I'm exhausted. Alex don't look at me like that, you need to save your sperm for tomorrow."

Save my sperm, what the hell was she talking about? Anyway the domestic drama seemed to have subsided so it was probably a good time to quit while he was ahead.

Chapter 4
Slideshow Presentation

Bella was not in the mood for the presentation. She was exhausted from last night's sobbing and shouting and did not need Anthony's pre-show nerves. Bella had arranged to meet Anthony for breakfast. This would typically involve him drinking several shots of Expresso and smoking an equal number of fags. As usual he was late. Bella ordered a hot chocolate and muffin and waited.

"Naughty Anthony, late again. Clive hadn't ironed any of my shirts because he's over his writer's block so I had to go and buy one, sorry darling. God you look rough, is it the time of the month or what?"

"No, I'm just a bit knackered. You know it's busy right now sorting out all the arrangements for the music awards."

"Yes, tell me about it. I'm disappearing in a sea of red."

Bella knew he was referring to his unread emails. Bella felt she was disappearing in a sea of red of a different kind but could still manage to hold it together at work.

"I'll just do my bit, and defer any questions to you – okay?"

After a couple of expressos, Anthony declared he was ready for his audience and made a dramatic entrance into the lobby of the newly acquired record label.

Anthony's red stripes on his new shirt and lived in face was in stark contrast to the monochrome youths who languished around the lobby looking for their fag break mates.

Anthony strode into the boardroom and began schmoozing the assembled audience. It always amazed Bella how companies managed to drag people into presentations who had no real interest or input in the process. She guessed it was just who was available on the day. Bella looked around the room and knew the key stakeholder, the finance guy, was missing. This meant one of two things - either he was too busy and they were about to waste two hours or in typical music industry style, he was going to be late. Normally Bella would favour the latter option but considering her doctor's appointment, she couldn't do late.

Anthony was a master at working the room and soon had the miserable looking assistants laughing at his over camp manner. One of the more miserable ones explained that Giles was running late, not how late just late.

Forty-five minutes later Giles appeared. Bella hoped they wouldn't have many questions.

Bella obediently pushed all the right buttons so Anthony's graphs appeared when he waved his hands. Bella just hoped they could convince the miserable bastards that they could do the job and just leave.

Anthony managed to get through the presentation with only two people leaving the room due to urgent issues, i.e. due to urgent issue of boredom. Despite Bella's feedback, Anthony could never grasp that creative types did not want death-by-PowerPoint. They liked interaction and flip charts with coloured pens. Anthony would always insist on delivering his 40 slides word for word. God it was painful.

Bella glanced at the clock. They were one hour behind schedule and the Finance Director was just about to prove how important cost management was in their business. Pretty pointless when the assistants knew it was all a load of crap. If they were looking after one of the top artists they could do what the hell and spend what the hell they wanted. The corporate lecture commenced whilst the clock ticked.

Queue the questions. Bella had her answers off pat and rattled the same stock responses she'd used for the last eleven years and besides if she didn't get out of the meeting in the next 10 minutes, she was going to miss her appointment.

The meeting started to disperse as they all had urgent deadlines. Yeah right, thought Bella, more like they hadn't had enough caffeine or nicotine. Bella decided to make her excuses whilst Anthony tried to butter up Giles. Bella knew Anthony would have forgotten she had a Doctor's appointment and would be pissed off she was leaving before he had exited the building.

Tough. Bella raced to the nearest tube and ran down the escalators. She couldn't have gone through last night's dramas for nothing.

Chapter 5
Doctors Appointment

Bella arrived at the doctors bang on time. She was sweating like mad and could barely breathe. Alex who clearly had been waiting a while looked calm and grabbed her arm to pull her into the doctor's room.

Bella thought the receptionist had booked them in with the younger female doctor. Clearly not, judging from the elderly bow-tied doctor flicking through paperwork.

"Please take a seat Mr and Mrs Moore. What can I do for you?"

Alex immediately looked at Bella. It looked like she would have to take control.

"Er… we have been trying for a baby for the last two years and er… we have not had any success."

"Okay, Mrs Moore have you ever been pregnant or had a baby?"

"No."

"And you Mr Moore?"

"Sorry?"

"Have you fathered any children?"

"No." Alex wondered where all this was going. Was he gathering details on Alex's sexual history or their inability to conceive?

"Mrs Moore, are your periods regular?"

"Yes, every 28 days."

"Have you had any major operations?"

"No."

"Fine, do either of you smoke?"

"No," they replied in unison.

"Alcohol, how many units do you each consume on a weekly basis?"

Bella looked at Alex who mumbled, "I think we are both within the Government guidelines."

Yeah right, thought Bella, Alex bloody wasn't.

"On a good week," piped up Bella.

"Okay, Mrs Moore in a typical week how many units do you consume?"

Bella averaged 2 G&Ts a night plus about 6 glasses of wine a week, so about 20 she reckoned. Bugger it she'd tell him 14.

"About 14, I think."

"And I have about 22," said Alex.

Bella knew this was complete crap. He'd had that in the last 24 hours. Bella knew better than to correct Alex in front of the doctor so she let it go.

"Okay, we can do some initial tests at the surgery but I will need to refer you to a fertility specialist who you can see once we have the results of your initial tests. Mrs Moore, you need to come into the surgery and have a blood test and Mr Moore, we need you to do a sperm test. I will provide a receptacle and you will need to drop it into Outpatients at Stevenson Hospital. You will need to ensure that the sperm is dropped in straight after it is collected and kept warm in transit. Dr Bunde is based at the Stevenson. I can either write to him and establish his waiting list on the NHS or you could call his secretary and arrange a private consultation."

Bella didn't like the sound of a waiting list. She got Alex this far and she didn't want any further delays.

"Could we have the phone number for his secretary please and we'll book a private consultation?"

Alex glared at Bella. Sod him, thought Bella, she'd pay.

"Do you have any questions?"

Alex looked at Bella.

"Can you just tell us about the tests and what you would expect to find?"

"Mrs Moore fertility investigations can take time and in a number of cases we are unable to find any medical reason why you are unable to conceive. You need to think of this as the start of the process and not raise your expectations too high that a cause will even be found, let alone a solution."

Bloody great, thought Bella.

"Any more questions?"

Bella saw little point in asking any more questions and thanked the Doctor whilst Alex collected his pot.

Alex and Bella walked to the station.

"Well?" said Bella.

"Well what?"

"What did you think?"

"I thought it went pretty well really."

"Oh for God's sake Alex, we have come out of there none the wiser. Did he bother to ask how we are feeling about all this? What if my blood test confirms we can't have children? Does the receptionist just coolly inform me over the phone?"

"Oh come on Bella like he said it is just the start of the process, let's deal with the results when we have them."

"I'm calling Dr Bunde when I get back to the office Alex. Now we've started this process I want to get moving."

"Okay."

Bella and Alex jumped on their respective trains and travelled back to work.

After an abrupt conversation with Dr Bunde's secretary, Bella established the options were a 3-month wait on the NHS or a Saturday morning consultation in three weeks' time for £150. There was no way Bella was going to wait three months, so she booked the appointment and texted Alex with the date.

Bella drifted through the rest of the afternoon. Anthony notably had not been in contact so Bella knew he was still mad about her premature exit from the meeting. Bella had managed to secure an 8 a.m. appointment for her blood test the following week so hopefully she could scrape in for 9 a.m. so Anthony wouldn't know. Bella also needed to broach with Alex the issue of the timing of his sample.

⤶

Bella was surprised to see Alex home on time devoid of the smell of stale beer. Bella was even more surprised that Alex declined wine at dinner. They had just settled down on the sofa to watch TV when the phone went. After a quick debate on who was going to answer the phone, Bella grabbed it.

"Oh, Hi Jen"

"Yeah, fine thanks, and you?"

Bella then listened to Jen's breakdown of pregnancy woes, including her food aversions and daily sickness schedule. Jen seemed to have been constantly pregnant for the last 4 years, and seemed to moan more with each conception. Guy and Jen were making no secret of the fact that number three was a slip up - just what Bella wanted to hear right now. Bella was genuinely fond of Jen and Guy. They had been married two years longer than she and Alex. Alex knew Guy plus his string of past conquests since meeting him and their other friend Andrew at University. They had all welcomed Bella straight away into the inner circle and whilst Jen could be rather direct, she meant well.

"How did you get on at the doctor's? I was surprised when Guy told me I thought you two didn't want kids, you know, with all the free travel you get."

Bella caught her breath. Bloody Alex! Bella could barely talk to Alex about this let alone anyone else. She wasn't ready for this.

Raising her voice, Bella glared at Alex

"Well now you know Jen, two years, no baby."

"Can the doctor do anything or can you just not have them?"

"We don't know yet, we just need to you know start the process and have some tests."

"Well, don't lose hope, I mean look at me during the 80s darling I was a total tart, never used contraception, honestly it was like Russian roulette, must have all fired blanks 'cos I never got pregnant. Then I met Guy, came off the pill four years ago and got pregnant with Maddie straight away. I swear Guy only has to look at me mid-cycle and my eggs fertilise, so like I say, don't give up all hope."

Bella wasn't sure what she was to take from this. Was Jen suggesting that Bella should sleep with Guy, or dump Alex and sleep with a few blokes until one got her pregnant?

Before Bella had the chance to respond, there was a shriek at the end of the phone.

"Look darling got to go, Maddie for God's sake, bloody hell she's put a ping pong ball in Jack's mouth. She's a total cow at the moment. Got to go, remember we're here for you."

Bella heard the line click and saw Alex slump on the sofa with a rather large whisky.

"Sorry Bella, I did mean to tell you I mentioned our situation to Guy."

"Oh right, that will be why Jen called to suggest I sleep with her husband in the name of getting pregnant then."

"What? I know she's pregnant but has she totally lost it? I'll talk to Guy he needs to know she's gone bloody mad."

"No need, she was just trying to be helpful. I just wasn't ready to talk about it with other people, Alex, and I wish we'd talked about this first."

"Surely you've talked about it with the girls."

"No Alex I haven't. Look, I'm knackered. It's no big deal that Guy and Jen know but can we just keep it at that for now, I mean even my parents don't know."

"Yeah sure, but I am really concerned that Jen is suggesting that you sleep with Guy."

"I think she was joking."

"She bloody better have been."

Chapter 6
Sperm Sample

Bella had managed to fit in her mid-cycle blood test and now needed to broach the fact with Alex that his sperm sample receptacle remained empty other than a few cat hairs accumulated when Ginger decided to paw it around the bedside table.

Alex had in fairness been on his best behaviour since their row before the doctors visit and Bella really didn't want to push him but Dr Bunde needed the test results and they were due to visit him in two weeks' time. Luckily, Anthony was in Miami allegedly checking out the accommodation for the music awards. The fact he had Clive in tow who apparently was researching the art deco buildings for his novel made it less convincing that he wasn't on yet another jolly. With Anthony prancing up and down Miami Beach without a tri-band phone, work was incredibly peaceful and there were plenty of opportunities for sneaking off to drop Alex's sample in. Tonight was the night. Bella decided to ensure Alex did his sample in the morning and she would take it into the hospital first thing.

Once again Alex arrived in from work sober and in a relatively good mood.

"Alex, I can take your sample into the hospital tomorrow if you like. We need to have the results by the time we see Dr Bunde."

"Oh great – no pressure."

"Come on I've had my blood test, like you said we're in this together."

"I was going to leave it another week, that's all."

"We might not have the results back in time. Why do you need to delay until next week?"

"No reason."

"So you'll do it in the morning then?"

"If you want the result to be crap, then I'll do it tomorrow."

"What do you mean, want the result to be crap?" Bella was becoming increasingly frustrated with this conversation; surely producing one in the bathroom was hardly an issue.

"Well I spoke to Guy and we figured out that if I maybe abstained from alcohol for a couple of weeks it might, you know, improve the results."

Bella could not believe Alex and Guy had been plotting a strategy to maximise sperm quality.

"For God's sake Alex, since when has Guy been some sort of sperm guru? I think you'll find you needed to stop drinking about three months ago. This process is about trying to find out if we have any problems and resolving them, not bloody hiding them. Just fill the pot Alex."

Bella decided to go to bed and paint her nails. Alex was bound to stay well clear when he smelt the fumes from the polish. Bella was angry. Why did he have to make everything so bloody difficult?

Bella woke to the sound of Alex cursing in the bedroom.

"Bloody Ginger, what's wrong with this cat? He's had the pot, little sod."

"I told you not to leave it on the side. It's probably under the bed."

After about 10 minutes of scrabbling under the bed with Ginger, Alex appeared triumphantly with the pot and disappeared into the bathroom. Bella jumped into the shower and quickly got herself ready, as she needed to ensure the sperm was kept warm until it reached the hospital.

"Here you go."

"Is that all?"

"How much do you think we need Bella? You really know how to make a man feel good."

Bella grabbed the sample and shoved it down her bra.

"What do you think you are doing with that?"

"Keeping it warm Alex. Now if you don't mind, I need to get to the hospital"

Bella drove like a mad woman to the hospital and raced to the reception.

She was met by a jolly looking man who looked like he had been helping himself to the drugs cabinet.

"I need to drop a sample in."

"Morning, bit chilly out isn't it, take a seat please dear."

"No, I need you to take it now, it's, you know, warm."

"Got you dear. Wendy can you pop to the lab the lady's got a hot pot."

God, did he have to be so loud, most of the waiting room looked at Bella expectantly as she produced the pot from the inside of her bra. Great.

Bella raced to work and spent the day wrapped up in the plans for the music awards. Bella's mobile buzzed with a call from Alex.

"Did you do it?"

"Yeah, it was quite embarrassing really especially when I produced the pot from the inner sanctum of my brassiere."

Alex laughed, "Glad you're in good spirits. You haven't forgotten we are going to Jen and Guy's tonight have you?"

Oh no, Bella had forgotten. She had been so tied up with the whole sperm thing she had forgotten it was the last Friday of the month and in time-honoured tradition they would get together with Jen and Guy and Andrew and Susannah. This ritual went back to when Alex, Guy and Andrew graduated and pledged to stay friends and ensure they always went out at least one night a month, the last Friday of every month. It had always remained as agreed. Andrew was absent for a few years whilst living in New York but they continued to meet and eventually Jen, Bella and then Susannah were introduced into the circle.

Bella just wasn't in the mood for it. She loved seeing Jen and Guy as they were always great fun but Andrew and his wife were a bloody pain.

Andrew had managed to become a Managing Director of an American Investment Bank, net himself an heiress to some USA clothing emporium and completely disguise the fact he originated from a council estate in Cardiff.

Susannah was his ultimate trophy wife. They met on a flight from New York to London and married a year later. Susannah clearly hated the monthly gatherings but Andrew would never miss an opportunity to flaunt his success to Guy and Alex.

Andrew had always been jealous of Alex's upbringing, purely on the basis that Alex's mother had a country pile, clearly forgetting the fact that Alex's father died when he was nine and he lived with his batty old mother who struggled to manage both Alex and his brother and run a huge house that she refused to part with.

Bella had met Andrew's parents. They occasionally came to stay when Susannah was out of town, and both

Bella and Alex thought they were lovely people. Andrew's Dad had taken early retirement from his job in the factory and his Mum made really nice cakes for special occasions. In fact, she had done Alex and Bella's wedding cake and refused to be paid a penny.

Andrew had totally lost his accent and even managed to retain a fake mid-Atlantic drawl when pissed which was truly remarkable. Since Michael Douglas married Catherine Zeta-Jones, Susannah had suddenly become very interested in Wales and repeatedly corrected her American friends when they referred to Andrew as being English. So far Andrew had managed to keep Susannah away from his parent's house but she was apparently begging him to take her to Wales for Christmas ever since she read that Michael and Catherine had allegedly done Christmas in Wales.

Bella decided to leave work early and make an effort to look good for the monthly nightmare, Susannah always made Bella feel like she had been dragged through a hedge backwards and she didn't need to feel any more inadequate than she already did.

"You look nice, very Britney Spears," Alex quipped.

Bella had washed her hair and managed to squeeze into some hipsters and a tight top.

"Yeah right, no doubt the Manhattan Princess will make me feel like a post menopausal Britney."

"Take no notice, she always looks so fake."

Fake in Bella's world was another word for perfect. Oh well, at least Jen would look a mess. She seemed to live in over sized jogging pants since she had been in a permanent state of pregnancy.

Chapter 7
Sad Cow in the Corner

Bella decided they would take a taxi to Jen and Guy's. Now that Alex had produced his sample he seemed keen to have a drink. Bella needed a drink to get through the evening with the Manhattan Princess.

They arrived at the war zone. Jen and Guy's place was in a right state. Maddie, their three year old, seemed to have replaced her Barbie pyjamas with a tutu and was thudding round the hall in the name of ballet, whilst Jake, their one year old, was howling in surround sound, partly through the floor and partly through the baby monitor.

In the middle of this Jen was trying to cook roast lamb and peel the potatoes, whilst throwing up at 10 minute intervals.

Guy was slumped in his chair in the lounge with a gin and tonic.

"Hi, glad to see you made it as far as the lounge, bloody nightmare here tonight – Jen for God's sake, has that baby monitor got a mute button on it?"

"That's not really the idea darling, do you want me to go and get him?"

"No I don't, we tried to get the kids in bed for seven so we could have a remotely civilised dinner, I'm sure they're psychic. Jen is it worth giving Jake some of that pink medicine stuff with the sedative in it?"

"He's not ill, Guy."

"I know he isn't but I will be if he doesn't shut up."

"Guy, you're really going to have to get him. He's been howling for 15 minutes now and I'm trying to cook a roast."

Bella was dying to go into the nursery and cuddle Jake, nuzzle up to him in his baby pyjamas with the feet in and smell his baby smell. Should she offer? What would Jen and Guy think? They knew about her inability to get pregnant. Would they push her out of the way and grab him just in case she turned into the character out of 'Hand That Rocked The Cradle?'

Sod it, they're friends, she was starting to get paranoid. She would normally help Jen out with the kids, what was different now? The fact they knew she couldn't get pregnant that's what the bloody difference was.

"Don't worry Jen if you're busy in the kitchen, I'll get him for you."

Jen bolted out of the kitchen. Bloody hell, thought Bella, she thinks I'm going to kidnap him.

"Don't worry about Jen, she's gone to be sick again. It's the only time she gathers speed, quite fast when she gets going considering the lack of traction her slippers have on the wooden floors. It would be great if you could grab Jake for us, I'm going to sort the drinks out."

Bella ran upstairs and opened the nursery door. Jake was sat in his cot red faced and sobbing, immediately he smiled. Bella lifted him out of the cot and cuddled him. He repaid her with a huge grin and an excited bounce. Bella stood holding him and tried to fight back the tears.

"I want to be a mummy so much," she whispered to Jake.

Bella decided to return quickly to the war zone to avoid any suspicion about her pretending to be a mummy in the nursery.

Bella was halfway down the stairs when Andrew and Susannah made their grand entrance.

Andrew had the annoying habit of wearing work shirts with jeans and loafers, trying to look as if he had perfected the casual but not scruffy look. Susannah was wrapped in another little cashmere ensemble. Bella took a second look at Susannah. Actually she didn't look as perfect as usual, she looked quite ill.

"Look at you Bella, it suits you. Always said to Alex, Bella's got great breeding hips."

In other words, Andrew always thought she was a fat cow.

Sensing Bella was riled, Guy put his arm around her.

"She's a natural alright, Jake was screaming the house down five minutes ago."

Bella wished they would just change the subject. She noticed Alex had virtually downed a tumbler of scotch since she'd emerged with Jake.

"No I'm not, I think Jake would respond well to the Child Catcher he just seems to want to join the party, must get it from you Guy, er what do you want me to do with him now?"

"God knows, is Jen still throwing up?"

"No, I've finished thank you, it's just the smell of the food."

"Good Lord Jen, do you have to put people off? I know you're no Fanny Craddock but it can't be that bad."

"It's just a pregnancy thing, Bella could you do me a favour and take him in the lounge, read him a couple of books and shove him back in his cot."

Bella shuffled into the lounge with Jake who was simply loving the chaos downstairs. Guy had been ordered by Jen to de-tutu Maddie and get her into bed. Everyone else was in the kitchen with Jen whilst Bella sat quietly with Jake and his books. Jake was cooing at a picture of a baby in one of his books when Alex walked in. Slowly he sat down in the corner with another scotch.

"Stop staring at me Alex," Bella hissed.

"I can't help it. Andrew's right, you are a natural."

"What, you think I'm a fat cow as well do you?"

"No, you know it's just seeing you there with a baby. What if my results come back and I can't, you know, make babies with you?"

"This is not the place to discuss this. I don't want everyone to know, plus as the doctor said it's early days so let's just take it one day at a time."

"I'm going to put Jake in his cot now. Just act normal Alex, for God's sake"

Bella hoped Alex was not going to get completely wrecked tonight. Since submitting his sperm sample he had been acting rather strangely.

Jake decided to be on his best behaviour for the Child Catcher and snuggled down into his cot. Bella decided to take in the baby smell once more before beating a hasty retreat. But what was that smell? Bella looked down at a pile of full nappy sacks, gross. Bella picked them up and trudged down to the kitchen.

"Jake's fine, I found a nest of dirty nappies on the floor. Where do you want them?"

Andrew immediately piped up "Look everyone told you how good she is she can even handle the crap."

Bella noticed Susannah was looking even paler and excused herself, probably the thought of baby poo.

"Just lob them out the back door. Guy will sort them later, thanks love."

In the middle of all the chaos both children actually went to bed and Jen managed to produce a meal.

Bella found herself drifting in and out of the various conversations and counting how many refills Guy had poured Alex now he was hitting the red wine.

Suddenly Andrew stood up as if to make a grand announcement.

"Sorry to break up the party but Susannah and I have an announcement to make, refill your glasses guys"

Bloody hell, thought Bella, she's sodding pregnant. She quickly stole a look at Susannah's cashmere encased stomach, which on cue she was rubbing and looking even smugger than ever. Why do pregnant women have to incessantly rub their stomachs? At least she was too classy to go the full measure and wear a 'baby on board' or 'here's one we made earlier' t-shirt. Jen shrieked with excitement whilst Guy stumbled round filling all of the glasses. Why didn't he just get on with it and tell everyone that she's sodding pregnant.

"My darling wife and I have some very exciting and unexpected news."

"You're getting divorced?" shouted Guy.

Susannah glared at Guy.

"On the contrary my dear friend, we are expecting our first baby."

The table fell silent. Bella knew Jen and Guy were trying to not look directly at her. What did they expect her to do, run out of the room sobbing or scratch Susannah's eyes out? This is why she didn't want people to know, bloody Alex.

"Well, aren't you going to congratulate us?"

"Of course" said Bella "I just didn't think you were you know interested in starting a family, but it really is great news. Congratulations to you both."

Once Bella had endorsed it was okay for Susannah to be pregnant and she wasn't about to boil her cashmere jumper, everyone quickly jumped in with kisses and the appropriate shrieks of excitement. Alex, on the other hand, was too pissed to notice.

Bella knew the rest of the evening was a write off. Cue the pregnancy and baby talk. She couldn't leave without it looking obvious. She was going to have to listen to them moaning on about pregnancy sickness. If Bella ever felt sick she would feel a tingle of excitement until the reality would dawn that more than one bottle of wine always made her sick.

"How many weeks are you?" shrieked Jen.

"We just had our 12 week scan. I'm actually 13 weeks"

"Fantastic, we'll be due within a few weeks of each other," said Jen.

Bella waited for the scan pictures to be produced, as Exhibit A. Without wanting to be completely bitter and twisted, Bella wondered why pregnant women feel the need to produce unidentifiable grey grainy pictures of aliens out of their handbags. Oh God, she was getting them.

"My obstetrician has a special 3D scanner, the pictures are just fab."

Andrew snatched the pictures.

"See you can tell he's going to be a looker, just like his mother."

Hopefully not a tosser like his father, Bella snarled under her breath.

"Do you have any scan photos Jen?"

"Er no, Jake got them out of my bag at the hospital and licked the print off them"

Guy butted in "Yes we nearly had to take the little sod to A&E. Jen didn't notice he had licked them and his mouth had gone blue. We thought he had stopped breathing."

Susannah gave one of her fake smiles.

"It's all been a bit of shock really, I mean with me being early thirties we didn't expect to get pregnant straight away."

Bella realised she was starting to down the regularly topped up wine. Early thirties yeah right, maybe after several sessions of Botox. The lying cow was at least 36. Expect to get pregnant straight away, why was it necessary for everyone she knew who was pregnant or had been pregnant to bleat, "We didn't expect it to happen straight away" or "our third was a bit of a mistake." Hang on, you're not taking any bloody contraception and you didn't expect to get pregnant, give every infertile couple in the world a break will you.

"It's all been quite stressful really because the birth was going to clash with Andrew's annual Managing Director's conference, but it's all sorted now."

At this point Bella became a little confused.

"Have the bank moved the conference then?"

"No darling my obbie is going to do a c-section at 38 weeks so Andrew doesn't miss it."

"Miss what, the birth?" asked Bella.

"No, the conference silly."

Bella excused herself and stumbled off to the loo just as Jen and Susannah were comparing the stresses of being pregnant.

Bella bumped into Guy on the landing who was checking on Jake.

"Are you okay?"

"Yeah fine, why wouldn't I be?"

"Well it must be difficult, you know with the old test results pending, especially with her bleating on about her "obbie". Stupid cow, would love to see her post birth complete with disposable crunchy knickers and baby sick."

Bella laughed. "I'm fine honestly, I just want people to act normally around us. I don't want to be the sad cow in the corner who can't get pregnant."

"Look we feel bad you know, we had no idea."

"It's fine, I really don't want Andrew and Susannah to know, in fact you and Jen are the only people who know."

"Fine by us, you know if you need anything we'll be there."

Jake started howling.

"Mind you, you may not want to use my sperm, Jen's always blamed me for Jake's ability to ruin a girl's evening."

Bella decided it was time to leave. Alex was starting to sift through Guy's CD collection and was showing all the signs of wanting to party. Bella knew negotiating their exit would be tricky. Alex was bound to accuse her of breaking up the party and would start acting like a naughty child.

"Alex time to go darling, I'm really tired."

"No."

Why did Alex insist on behaving like a petulant toddler after a few drinks? Bella decided to manhandle him out of the door whilst kissing everyone goodbye and apologising for Alex who was playing an air guitar to a lamppost.

Bella grabbed a cab and Alex immediately fell asleep. Bella knew she would end up putting him to bed, and she wanted another baby?

Chapter 8
Test Results

Bella felt rough from too much red wine. It was going to be one of those wasted weekends when they both felt too hung-over to do anything.

Alex rolled over.

"Ergh, I feel rough."

"I'm not really surprised, you were mixing scotch and wine again love."

"Did you enjoy it?"

"Well I did up until the Manhattan princess eclipsed into the pregnant princess."

"What are you talking about?"

"Alex, Susannah is pregnant, she produced 3D pictures of an alien from her handbag and drawled on about her c-section being scheduled around Andrew's conference."

"Is she, did she, wow. Guy must have been heavy handed with the top ups. I had no idea."

"It was horrible. Jen and Guy just stared at me after Andrew did his grand announcement and I felt really awkward. That's why I didn't want people to know. I'm also worried they won't want me to babysit any more."

"What the hell are you talking about?"

"I didn't want anyone to know Alex. I just feel people will view me differently, as Bella, the sad cow in the corner who can't get pregnant and by the way don't let her near the children's playground in case she tries to snatch one."

"Don't be ridiculous nobody is going to think that. Okay we are struggling to have a baby but it hasn't changed you as a person."

"No, but I think it will change people's view of me and of us. I don't want anyone tip toeing around me Alex, you know, frightened to tell me if they're pregnant or thinking that keeping their baby away from me is going to help. If people have to know I just want them to treat me normally. I felt really isolated last night. We are going to be the only childless couple in our group of friends and I'm finding it really hard. I'm pleased for Andrew and Susannah but when I hear Susannah moaning about being sick and how difficult it was to find an obbie and how she didn't expect to get pregnant straight away, I wanted to punch her lights out."

"You've never been like this with Jen. This is Jen's third pregnancy and you've been fine."

"I can't explain it Alex. I feel it's okay for Jen to be pregnant. She's a great mum and I love the kids to bits, but Susannah…she'll have done it on the back of the latest yummy mummy fashion splash in 'OK'. I don't think she deserves it."

"Bella, how on earth can you judge who deserves to get pregnant? I know Susannah can be a total cow but she is pregnant and we're going to have to deal with it. If you feel angry and resentful, the only person that's going to suffer is you and I don't want that. You've always been so strong"

"I know, it's since we started the tests Alex. Before I would think well never mind it could be me next month. Now I'm thinking how the bloody hell we will deal with not being able to have any children if the test results reveal a problem."

"We'll get through it Bella and as you said to me last night, we are not at that point yet. It's the start of a process that's all."

"I need a fry up."

Bella felt sick, both sick from too much wine and emotionally sick rolled into one. She opened the curtains, God it was bright outside. She noticed the flashing light from the answerphone and hit play.

"Alex, did you check the answerphone before we went out last night?"

"Bella I got ready in ten minutes. I didn't even look at it. Why what's happened?"

"Our test results are back. Apparently we need to phone into the doctor's surgery individually and they'll give them to us over the phone. They're open until 12 noon. Oh God, Alex, what do we do?"

"Call them, Bella, what's the alternative?"

"I'm just too hung-over today Alex. Shall we call on Monday?"

"Bella if you think I'm discussing my sperm test results with a doctor whilst on the trading floor on a Monday morning, you must still be pissed."

"I feel really sick, are you going to speak to them first? What if your results are okay and mine aren't?"

"I'm phoning them now, I'll speak to them first, I'm not going to spend hours agonising over this. My sperm has been analysed Bella and I want to know the results. If I've been firing blanks all these years I want to damn well know... er yes hello it's Mr and Mrs Moore here. I believe you have some test results for us? Yes I have a pen."

Alex seemed to be writing for ages. What the hell was going on?

"What does all that mean? Well, it sounds horrendous. Bella, when are we seeing the baby doctor person?"

"Next Saturday."

46

"Look, we're not seeing the specialist until next week. Get a doctor on the phone I need to understand these results."

Bella snatched the piece of paper.

Alex had distractedly doodled tadpoles all around the scribbled note that read:

'Sperm Count normal = 70 million per mil
Motility only moderate (50% @ 3 hrs)
Abnormal forms 40%'

What did that all mean? Bella held Alex tightly while he waited for the doctor's explanation.

"Well, it didn't look okay to me, so what you're saying is 'could do better.' It doesn't mean we can't have kids. Okay, I'll put you onto Bella."

Bella could really do without this today. Her head was pounding. The doctor calmly informed her that the blood tests they had taken mid-month were normal.

"Are you okay Bella?"

"I think so, my test results were normal."

"Oh great, it could be me then? Apparently I haven't got a gold star. More like a C minus and then the patronising git told me my slightly below average results were down to age and lifestyle and could be improved. For God's sake Bella you know I hardly touched a drop for three weeks before that damn test."

"Alex, this is good news. We're past the initial tests. Mine are okay and let's talk to the specialist about yours. It might be if you stop drinking yours will be fine as well."

"I hoped I'd fair better than this. Look how much Guy drinks. He's my age and they don't have any problems. How come people father kids when they are alcoholics or on drugs? I just have a few drinks to get me through the week and my results are crap."

"Alex, it's not a competition. Yours obviously need a little more work."

"Thanks, I'm going back to bed."

Bella didn't feel she'd handled that at all well. What was this whole macho pride thing attached to his sperm test? It didn't seem good enough for Alex that the results could be improved. He wanted to be Mr Super Sperm. This was going to be harder than she thought. She wondered if the baby man would be able to calm Alex down and reassure him of his virility. It was only another week and it felt like the box of infertility secrets had been opened. Her previous reluctance to know what was going on was replaced by a need to urgently gain information. Bella wondered if Alex fully understood the lifestyle changes they were probably going to have to make. They'd made a half-hearted attempt at not drinking before and cutting down on takeaways when Bella joined a programme on maximising fertility through natural methods. After two months of seriously reduced alcohol, foul smelling tea and copious amounts of brown rice they took the edge off the arrival of her second period by drinking two bottles of wine and eating a kebab. Roll on Saturday.

Chapter 9
Clinical Exam

Bella was having a really bad week at work. Anthony was back from Miami and one of their clients had been arrested at Heathrow for punching a member of staff at the gate when the aircraft left without them and, guess what? It was Bella's fault. Bella and Anthony were due to meet with the client's PR people who were trying to put a positive spin on the punching incident. Bella had been through this before with clients and needed to feed Anthony the correct lines so "Useless Travel Agent Causes Punch Up At Heathrow" did not appear in tomorrow's papers.

"Morning Darling, God I'm stressed, bloody flight was overbooked so we ended up down the back with children. It's about time they did something about children on flights, I mean they managed to sort out smoking. On long haul flights they should stick all the kids on the upper deck with a clown and lock the door. What the hell are we going to say to these PR people?"

"It's quite simple, Anthony, we cannot hold a 747 at Heathrow because one of our clients is too hung-over to get out of bed. I called the airline, told them he was going to be late and explained to his assistant's assistant that the flight could not be held and unless he was at the gate twenty minutes before, it would leave without him."

"So what happened?"

"The assistant's assistant was too scared to tell him as he was already in the process of assaulting the driver on the way to the airport so she told him I had ensured the aircraft would be held at Heathrow."

"Do assistants have assistants these days then?"

"Apparently so, Anthony, you just need to tell the PR people the truth so they can make up a completely different story."

"Okay, good I'll handle this. Bella, you stay at your desk like a good girl we don't want any more cock ups."

Great, he also thought it was her fault. What a week, Alex had spent most evenings on various Internet health websites, clutching his sperm test results and his balls, convinced he was ill. Alex made this self-diagnosis on the basis that Guy drank more than him and had managed to get Jen pregnant three times.

Anthony met with the PR people and they all decided it was better not to implicate a third party and as their client's album was due to be released in six months' time, they thought he should have a breakdown tomorrow and check into a clinic in the States. At the time of his album release he would be fully recovered and his interviews would be more interesting as he could describe the pain of his breakdown and his sorrow over the incident at Heathrow – perfect.

Bella and Alex had barely seen each other all week. Alex was either at work or on the Internet and Bella was either at work or reading her infertility survival guide – again.

Saturday rolled round very quickly. Bella immediately felt sick when she woke up. Alex was already pacing round the bedroom.

"So what time are we going to see the baby doctor?"

"Alex, please don't call him that. We need to leave in 45 minutes. What the hell are you wearing?"

In the half light of the bedroom Bella could see Alex was wearing an old pair of tie-dyed cotton trousers bought when he was drunk at a beach party in Koh Samui 10 years ago.

"I've been trying to find these for an hour. I need to wear this sort of thing from now on without pants, obviously not on the trading desk but certainly in leisure time."

"Bloody hell Alex, have you joined some strange cult? It's the middle of winter and you're not going to the hospital like that. They'll have you sectioned."

"So you aren't going to support my programme to improve my sperm count then? I need to reduce the temperature down below, you know, no hot baths, no underwear, I'm sure it will help."

"I'm sure it will Alex but for God's sake put your jeans on, can we just find out what is wrong first before you start wearing tie-dyed beachwear in Clapham in February?"

Reluctantly, Alex agreed to wear his jeans and then moaned all the way on the tube that he was too hot.

Dr Bunde greeted them at Outpatients and took them to his office. Bella was instantly struck by the pictures of babies all over the office walls. Wasn't that a bit insensitive?

"Right then Mr & Mrs Moore, I'm just going to quickly check the scanning room is free so I can do a quick scan for Mrs Moore. I'll be back in a moment."

"Er, sorry I think we're in the wrong place, Bella isn't pregnant, I can't get her pregnant er.. I mean we can't get pregnant."

"It's not a scan to look at a baby, Mr Moore, I just want to have a quick look at Mrs Moore's reproductive organs, back in a jiffy."

"Oh great start Alex, well done."

"Well how the hell did I know? I thought you only had scans when you were pregnant."

"Never mind, what do you think about having all the baby pictures on the wall. It's a bit insensitive isn't it? I mean what if he scans me and my reproductive organs are screwed so to speak, we can't have kids and he brings me back to a room of bouncing baby photos to tell me."

"Don't be ridiculous Bella. He's only promoting his work. It's just like going to the hairdressers, you know, when they have pictures of the different styles of haircuts around."

"It is nothing like going to the bloody hairdressers Alex. We don't get to say 'we'd like that one could you do it this morning?'"

Their argument was interrupted by the return of Dr Bunde.

"So then Mr & Mrs Moore, I understand from your Doctor's referral that you have been trying for a baby for two years without success. Neither of you has had a child in the past. Mrs Moore, you have never been pregnant and there is no medical history to explain your inability to conceive."

Nicely summed up thought Bella, i.e. we don't have a bloody clue why you can't get pregnant.

They both nodded.

"Have you seen my sperm test results? I really don't get it, I mean compared to my mate I don't get that drunk and he's managed to get his wife pregnant three times. Do you think there could be something wrong with me?"

Bella could not believe he had started going on about his sperm. They had only been there five minutes.

"Mr Moore, the conception process is very complicated and before we can reach any conclusions I need to do a number of tests. I have reviewed your sperm test results and would suggest with some considerable lifestyle changes they could be improved, but I would like have a full picture before we discuss likely causes of infertility. "

Bella decided to take over.

"Could you talk us through the tests, potential outcomes and how you fix any problems?"

"Okay, firstly you need to understand that we may go through all of the tests and find no medical reason why you can't conceive. This is known as unexplained infertility. It affects 20-25% of all infertile couples. If this is the case you can either continue leaving it to nature or considering your ages, Mrs Moore, I understand that you are 32 and Mr Moore, you are 42, I would suggest you look at starting fertility treatment. If we do find a medical reason to explain your infertility then we would need to decide medically if you are suitable candidates for fertility treatment."

It all sounded a bit vague to Bella.

Oh God, Alex was about to speak.

"How quickly will we know?"

Obviously desperate to clear his own name, thought Bella.

"I suggest I initially scan Mrs Moore this morning. I will then talk you through the fertility treatment options. Mrs Moore will then need some blood tests and when I have those I suggest we meet again and discuss the options. This will also give you time to consider the fertility treatment options."

"I've already had my blood tests," said Bella.

"I can see the GP has done some blood work but you also need a test on day two of your period. When is your period due?"

"Tuesday."

"Excellent, well on the basis that your cycles appear to be regular I'll give you a form and you can pop along on Wednesday and then my secretary will call you to book an appointment to discuss the results."

More time off work thought Bella, great.

"Right, let's go and have a quick look at you, Mrs Moore. Mr Moore just wait here."

Dr Bunde took her through the maze of corridors until they reached the scan room. In the adjacent waiting room a couple were sat both sobbing.

"I'll be with you in about 20 minutes."

They both looked up gratefully. Bloody hell what was going on? What had he just told them? Oh God, she wanted Alex.

"Just remove your trousers and underwear Mrs Moore and open your legs. I just need to set up the machine."

Bella really did not expect to be dropping her knickers on the first visit, it was freezing and as she laid back with her legs open she felt her knees starting to knock together. Dr Bunde produced this huge probe and a condom and started squirting jelly on it. Alex would love this. Thank God he was in the other room deciding which baby he wanted.

"Just relax, I'm just going to have a poke around."

How the hell could she relax in a freezing cold room with a complete stranger sticking a condom-covered probe up her. Suddenly the screen started to show lots of grey wobbly bits, which Dr Bunde started to point out.

"Left ovary, over a bit, over a bit more."

Ouch, thought Bella. I haven't got a right one. He can't find it.

"Over a bit, here we go, right ovary"

There was more shuffling below. He was muttering on about her uterus and staring intently at the screen. Bella scrutinised the scanner, could he see anything wrong? How the hell could he in that grey mass?

"Okay Mrs Moore you can get dressed."

Bella quickly got dressed. She'd rather hear any bad news with her knickers on, and thank God she'd put a decent pair on.

"It all looks fine to me. Bit difficult to judge on the scanner. You may need a laparoscopy to get a full picture but initially things look okay."

Hang on, thought Bella, I now need another test?

Bella and Dr Bunde quickly made their way back to Alex. She couldn't believe he was reading Dr Bunde's medical file, which he quickly threw back onto the desk.

"So has she got all the right bits?"

Thanks Alex.

"Yes, everything seems to be in order. If we are unable to find anything else as a result of our tests your wife may wish to have a laparoscopy which is an inspection of the pelvis using a small telescope. It is a simple procedure, and does not require a stay in hospital. We normally do it as a day case. You need to understand that there is a considerable waiting list on the NHS but privately we could sort you out in the next few weeks."

"Sorry, what's she got to have and how much is it?"

I'll refer you to my colleague who can discuss his fees directly with you".

Bella could see the pound signs flickering in Alex's eye.

"How long would we need to wait on the NHS?"

"At least 18 months. One option if the blood tests are okay is to go ahead with fertility treatment anyway. The only problem is we still would not have the full picture regarding your infertility. If you wanted to go ahead with treatment and you are suitable candidates we would maybe start with IUI, as it's less invasive. IntraUterine Insemination involves injecting your treated sperm into the uterine cavity via the cervix. We would normally use fertility drugs to increase the chances of success. If after say 3 cycles of IUI we hadn't succeeded and your infertility still couldn't be explained, we would normally recommend a move to IVF. In Vitro Fertilisation means that fertilisation will take place outside of your body in a glass. The process bypasses the fallopian tubes. Mrs Moore would take fertility drugs to stimulate her ovaries to produce follicles. Each follicle should contain an egg. We measure the size and quantity of the follicles via ultrasound scans throughout the treatment. At the appropriate time a final injection is given, normally 36-40 hours prior to egg collection and we then collect the eggs vaginally using ultrasound to guide us. The eggs are collected under general anaesthesia via a probe, an aspiration needle, which is passed via the vagina into the follicles. We then examine the fluid in our lab to identify the eggs. We never really know about the quantity or the quality of the eggs until we collect them. After collection, the eggs are incubated for a short time and the sperm is added. We then wait for fertilisation to take place. The fertilised eggs, or embryos I should say, are returned to the uterus 48-72 hours after collection. We limit the amount we transfer and discuss options for any surplus embryos with you. The transfer is a painless procedure that takes place via a transfer catheter placed within the uterine cavity. There follows a two-week wait to establish if the treatment has been successful. Again, there are waiting lists for this procedure that we would need to review once we decide how to proceed. Anyway let's wait for the next round of blood tests and we'll take it from there."

"More tests," sighed Bella as they waited for the lift.

"I know but do you really want to start any treatment without knowing where we stand? What's the average success rate of all this Bella, 15-20%? He's just trying to work out if we have sod all chance, that's all.

"Oh don't say that Alex. We need to try and be positive. It's just so clinical. I want someone to sit down with me and talk about the emotional side of all this. What if I have the laparoscopy and I can't have children, am I just informed in my post-operative state and left to pick up the pieces?"

"What do you expect Bella? Tea and sympathy? These guys are just doing their job and we need to be there emotionally for each other. We're on our own with this. We also need to talk about who we're going to tell."

"What do you mean?"

"Well if you need to have this operation and we need to have any treatment at least your parents and my mum should know, and you are going to need time off work so I guess Anthony will need to know."

Bella hadn't thought this through. Part of her wanted to keep it totally private, and the very thought of Anthony asking how her ovaries were doing during a meeting made her feel ill. Alex's mum wouldn't be a problem. She was completely in a world of her own. The loss of Alex's father had destroyed her and she roamed around their dilapidated house like some tragic character out of a Virginia Woolf novel. Alex's mum wouldn't even understand it let alone interfere. Her own parents' talk of her shooting up drugs and Alex's sperm count would certainly brighten up her mother's suburban coffee mornings. As for her father, he certainly wouldn't be prepared to discuss it because it would just be too personal but he would certainly be able to calculate all of the costs involved and probably tell them it was too expensive. Bella did actually love her parents and Alex got on well with them, which was a bit of a bonus, but their life was totally removed from theirs. Bella's father, typical accountant in suburbia and her mother, well she was a typical housewife in suburbia. Bella knew her mum would tell half the street and she made a mental note not to go home during any treatment cycles.

"I guess we'll have to tell them, at least it will liven mother's coffee mornings up."

Alex's phone beeped.

"Guy's just sent a text. I told him we were going to the baby doctor today, hope you don't mind?"

"What does it say?"

Alex showed Bella his phone.

how was it, did u have to do one in the cupboard? were magazines good? fancy a beer monday? G.

"Why would he want to know about the magazines? I didn't see any, did you?"

"He means the porn mags they supply in the cupboards to help you produce a sample."

"He's unbelievable. We're trying to find out if we can have children and Guy is trying to find out about the hospital's porn collection."

"It's a bloke thing. He's just curious and trying to find out how we got on. I'll text him back and tell him the hospital was fantastic and due to the fact we're going private they not only provide mags but videos too."

Chapter 10
Turkey Baster

Bella went for her blood test and they scheduled an appointment with Dr Bunde for the following Saturday. Bella agreed with Alex that she would help Jen with the kids whilst he and Guy had a night out in the city to review sperm counts. As usual, Bella was running late so she went straight round to Jen's after work and, as usual, it was chaotic.

Bella waited at least two minutes for Jen to open the door.

"So sorry love, God, I've had a bad day. We've all been to a tea party and my two were little sods. Jake kept throwing toys at other children and Maddie kept biting people. Come in, I've chilled some wine."

Bella dodged various pieces of plastic in the hallway and made it in one piece to the kitchen.

"Where are they?"

"In bed, totally knackered. I thought I would speed read their bedtime stories to them so we could have some time together to have a catch up. I've saved you some of the kid's spag bol and I'll just sort you some wine, if you're drinking that is? Guy reckons Alex is going to have to go on the wagon for a while, to sort out the old sperm count."

"I don't know Jen, quite possibly, we're just in the process of finding out if anything is wrong or if we're in the equivalent medical category of we haven't got a bloody clue why you can't have a baby."

"Really, you mean they don't always know."

"In about 20-25% of cases they don't."

"Can they treat you if they don't know what's wrong?"

"I guess they would just start us off on fertility treatment, sniffing and shooting up drugs etc. I think they'd probably start with IUI."

"Is that the one when you have all the drugs and then they use a turkey baster type thing?"

"Yes, that's the one. The baby would then be conceived inside you as opposed to having an out of the body experience in a petri dish somewhere."

"Do they have much success with that?"

"I think the IVF success rates are only around 20-25% for my age group and I would imagine IUI is even less. The difficulty is with IUI you could potentially end up with multiple babies, like you could with IVF but I think at my age with IVF they would only put two embryos back, with IUI multiple eggs could fertilise and you could end up with more than you bargained for."

"What on earth do they do about that?"

"I'm not really sure but to be honest I'm just tempted to go straight to IVF. The success rates are higher and I just want to give it the best shot. I'm waiting for my blood test results and then I'll probably need to have a laparoscopy to check all my bits are working then if it's okay I want us to go for IVF."

"How does Alex feel about it? What if you had twins? I mean it's a nightmare with one."

"Alex seems keener than ever. I think since he realised he's perhaps not Mr Super Sperm his desire to father a child has become more of a priority. I guess it's a man thing. I haven't even thought about twins Jen. I just want to get pregnant. I want a bump. I want to show off pictures of grey blobs to unknown strangers and I don't want to feel like this any more."

"Like what?"

"Like something in my life is missing and I'm a failure because I can't get pregnant. I know we are going to have to tell people and you and Guy have been fab but you will never know how this makes me feel. It bloody hurts Jen, every month feeling like a failure for the last two years, watching excited kids meet their Daddies off the train, hearing Susannah bleating on about scheduling her c-section, stuck in a traffic jams staring at bright yellow' baby on board' signs in the backs of cars. God I wish they'd make a 'sad infertile couple on board' sign. I'm sick of reading articles about these amazing women who juggle a full time career with raising kids. I haven't seen many articles about amazing women who juggle their career whilst going through IVF to have the bloody kids! I can't begin to tell you, and all this time we agreed not to talk to anyone about it, you know keep it between us and play it low key and all the time it's eating me up inside. It's like a grief that consumes you, like you are grieving for something you don't have and that you may never have. God, I'm sorry"

Bella started to sob. She grabbed a pack of spaghetti smeared tissues.

"Oh Bella, I'm so sorry. I had no idea, please don't cry. Have you tried taking time out just relaxing, you know you hear of so many couples falling pregnant when they go on holiday."

"We've tried the lot - special diets, stopping caffeine, cutting down on alcohol, taking holidays. I've even resorted to post-coital headstands and shoving pieces of crystal down my bra. We've done all that, still no baby."

"Bella, this isn't like you, you're normally such a fighter look what you have to put up with at work. Don't let this thing beat you."

"What do you mean?"

"You can do it, think of it as a challenge you know like one of your stupid things at work, like what do you say? Getting seat 1A, that's it, don't let it beat you, throw everything at it and you'll make it happen, you always do."

"So this is Bella vs. Infertility, round one is it, bring on the IVF."

"Go for it. I know it's already taken two years but you're grieving for something you haven't lost yet, if you allow yourself to become consumed in all that grief you are going to find IVF really tough. Take it one day at a time. You can't control the future but you can control how you deal with it. Fight it Bella, I know you can do this, don't give up now. I know we moan about the kids and they can be little sods but they enrich your life more than you can ever imagine and believe me they would be worth fighting for."

"What if I can't have children?"

"You don't know that, so don't try and deal with it. Right now you need to use all your energy to fight this Bella, if anyone can do it you can."

"You're right, I can do this, thanks Jen. I just needed some support and with Alex so wrapped up in his sperm count, I was losing the plot and you may have just saved me."

"And don't let Susannah get to you. She's in her world of C-sections, designer prams and cashmere blankets. She's hasn't bloody had one yet, a baby that is, she'll soon land when the designer pram won't fit in the boot and she's on her tenth visit to the dry cleaners to sort her puke stained cashmere blanket. Who are you going to tell?"

"At the moment it's just you and Guy. I think we'll tell Alex's mum and my parents and, wait for it, Anthony."

"Oh my God, can you imagine Anthony? He'll be working out how much time off you'll have if you produce triplets. I bet he'll think it's triple maternity leave. How will you get the time off for the laparoscopy and then potentially IVF?"

"Not sure. I'm not ill so I guess I'll have to try and juggle. I've got some holiday left if need be.

"It hardly seems fair. If you were pregnant you would have time off for all the scans and you could even go to ante-natal classes in the middle of the day and he could do sod all about it. Yet, you'll be taking annual leave to have IVF. Can't you just pretend you're sick?"

"I'd rather not. I'll get round it somehow, and you know maybe they'll have early appointments or something. I mean women work and do this don't they? I couldn't afford to give up my job and commit my life to getting pregnant. What if I never manage to conceive? Then it'll be no job and no baby. Forget that, I'll find a way round it."

"You know we're here for you. I know it's difficult because of the kids and I feel really guilty that we moan about them all the time but you can talk to us if you want."

"Thanks, do me a favour, and just treat me the same as you always did. I'd hate it if you felt you couldn't call the kids little sods or moan about your 24/7 sickness."

Bella was interrupted by a large thud in the hall. They both ran out of the kitchen to find Guy straddling a baby walker.

"Guy! What time do you call this? I nearly grabbed the bread knife. I thought we had burglars. It's 9 o'clock and you're never normally back before 2 a.m. when you've been out with Alex."

"Yeah, well, poor old chap's desperately trying to improve the old sperm count. He drank water all night and refused point blank to go into any busy bars in case they were too hot. He apparently had to leave early so he could take his pants off. No idea what that was all about. Mind you, if they manage to shake his sperm and your eggs around enough in the test tube to create a baby, then at least the old bugger will be back out on the razzle.

Jen glared at him.

"Just sod off to bed will you."

"I would if my leg wasn't stuck in this stupid lump of plastic. Baby walker, what a joke, he only uses it as a vehicle of mass destruction."

Jen patiently extracted Guy from the vehicle of mass destruction and helped him upstairs.

"Sorry about Guy. He's had a few too many."

"Don't worry Alex is normally ten times worse than that. Look, I better be off. I'll call you when I'm back from the baby doctor on Saturday. Thanks for tonight."

"That's okay, we're keeping everything crossed."

Chapter 11
Support Group

Bella actually felt a bit better. Jen was right, she could fight this. It had been eating away at her, making her feel less of a person and why should she allow herself to be damaged in this way? Okay, they might not be able to have children but she was not going down without a fight. It was baby doctor day again and they sat staring at various styles of baby on Dr Bunde's walls waiting for the baby maker to appear with the test results.

"Okay Mr & Mrs Moore, we have the test results and whilst this may not be the only factor, I think it's fair to say that the blood test results are well outside of the normal range for Mrs Moore's age."

Bella started to panic.

"What exactly do you mean?" asked Bella.

"I don't want you to leave this room with the idea that I'm saying you are going to go into an early menopause but your blood tests indicate that there is either a problem with the quantity of your egg reserve or the quality. The numbers are not high enough to demonstrate that you are in the menopause, but to be frank Mrs Moore these are the sort of test results I would expect to see from a 42 year old woman, not a 32 year old."

Bella was struggling to speak.

"Does this mean we can't have children?"

"No not at all. The numbers are not high enough to confirm you are in the menopause and you have regular periods. You do need to understand however that your success rates for IVF would be considerably lower than the average for your age group. If you do have a reduced egg reserve your body may not respond as well to the drugs involved with IVF treatment. Normally we prefer to collect a few eggs to maximise the chances of success and it may mean that you cannot produce enough eggs of a good enough quality to fertilise."

"What are my chances?"

"Difficult to say. The problem is until we try you with a cycle of IVF it is difficult to predict your chances of success."

Alex looked confused.

"Sorry for being thick, but if it is that my wife is running out of eggs, how long do we have?"

"Again, it's difficult to say, it could be a while or it could be a few months."

"Okay so if my wife does go into the menopause in a couple of months, what happens then? How can we have a baby?"

"Well there are ways Mr Moore, perhaps you would need to consider egg donation, but I suggest you try the drugs first so we can understand Mrs Moore's response to the treatment."

Bella could not get to grips with this. Alex grabbed her hand and held it tightly.

"I'm sorry, where would you get the eggs from?"

"Some clinics have egg share programmes where couples donate eggs to a pool of donors and you are placed on a waitlist until you have a match. This can take a considerable amount of time. It's not like sperm. There are no egg banks. It is illegal to pay egg donors in the UK so it is dependent on couples who are going through IVF who are prepared to donate some eggs in return for financial help with their own treatment or couples who have friends or family who are willing to donate or completely altruistic donors."

"Alex, it means the baby would be biologically yours but not mine."

"What? So I'd be having a baby with another woman. Bloody hell, oh sorry Doctor Bunde."

"Egg donation is an option that you would need to research fully and both take part in counselling sessions before you made any decisions, but I really don't feel we are at that point. I suggest we start by seeing how Mrs Moore responds to a cycle of IVF."

"What about my laparoscopy?"

"My advice would be to try the drugs first. It might be that you do have additional problems but let's see how you respond to the drugs."

"So I guess we would go straight to IVF."

"Yes Mrs Moore, I would advise that if you are able to produce a few eggs of a decent quality you go for IVF."

"When can we start?"

"Unfortunately you would not be considered ideal candidates for IVF under the guidelines we have for the area you live in. You do however have the option of paying privately. If you are able to pursue the private option then you can start straight away. Here are the fees involved."

Alex started to bristle.

"So what if we couldn't afford private treatment?"

"It wouldn't be possible for you to receive treatment immediately, even if you did meet the criteria there would still be a waiting list."

"Just as well we can stretch to it."

"Here's all the information and costs relating to private treatment. These hormone levels can bounce around a bit and we like to pick a good month for treatment. It would involve Mrs Moore coming in for blood tests at the start of each period so we can determine a month for treatment. I suggest that you think about it and call my secretary on Monday if you wish to go ahead. Obviously there are a number of alternative clinics that offer private treatment. If you did prefer to go ahead with another clinic I am more then happy to forward your notes so they have access to your investigations."

Dr Bunde gently ushered them out of his consulting room.

Bella was lost for words.

"Bella don't worry, we'll sort it."

"It's my fault Alex, we can't have a baby because either my eggs are crap or I'm running out of them. Oh my God, I thought there could be something wrong like a blocked tube or something they could fix, but not this. They can't do anything about this. We started trying for a baby two years ago. It's not like I was late thirties or early forties. I never expected to have this problem."

"Look, he said we can try IVF. Let's just go for it, you may well respond to the treatment and everything will be fine. What will we do about my sperm? I never asked him about that. According to an article I read it takes a few months to perk up if I go on the wagon. What if we're advised to go for it straight away?"

"Oh God, I forgot about your sperm."

"Great thanks, I'll look on the Internet to see if there are ways to give it an instant lift, you know Jordan's pictures always had that effect on me".

"Alex!"

"From what he's saying it might take a few months before your hormones are at the right level anyway."

"I'm really scared Alex."

"What is there to be scared of? We knew we would probably end up having IVF and like he said your periods are regular so it might just be that the drugs give you that boost you need and switch the old egg factory on. He hasn't actually said we can't have children. You're not in the menopause, don't be scared darling."

"I'm not scared about having IVF. I'm scared about failure and let's face it, the odds are crap."

"Well, put it like this, I've had worse on roulette and won. Remember when I won $1,000 in Vegas? You *can* beat the odds Bella."

"Great, so you're comparing my chances of getting pregnant to the night you got completely pissed on holiday and won on roulette... Baby roulette, an interesting concept Alex."

"It does happen."

"Don't talk to me about miracles. You know couples who have tried for 20 years to adopt children and suddenly get pregnant. All very interesting but I'll just wait for my own miracle, thanks."

"We'll look into clinics. We'll find the best, and give it our best shot. We've come this far and you might be panicking over nothing."

"At least we can afford to do this Alex, what about couples that can't? It's like you lose your reproductive rights if you can't pay for treatment. How the hell can you sit on a waiting list if you could tip into the menopause at any time? I know funding is stretched and there are more worthy causes but I bet the decision makers don't know how couples feel who might be facing a childless future. I don't even know how I feel now. Earlier I was confident I could fight this, now I'm just in bloody shock."

"We can fight this and we will. We'll look up clinics on the Internet and you'll have to call them on Monday.

Maybe there's a clinic that specialises in egg problems. Anyway what if Dr Bunde is wrong, or he hasn't got the latest technology. There might be other options and we need to come up with a code name."

"Sorry?"

"Well you're obviously going to have to call me at work and I don't think I'd ever live it down if I started discussing your egg reserve. I know we'll call it 'project roulette'. The boys will just think I'm gambling again."

"Whatever, I need to call Jen. I promised her an update."

Bella had to go through it all with Jen. She left the bit out about egg donation, and it really wasn't something she could get her head round at this stage. Jen was as supportive as humanly possible considering Guy had gone to watch the rugby and she was left with the terrible twosome.

Bella and Alex spent a quiet weekend scouring websites. Alex got quite excited at some of the 'babes' available on USA websites when he looked up egg donation. Apparently you could pay for donors over there and Ivy League blonde haired blue-eyed babes were at a high premium. Alex did suggest sending the link to Guy, Bella responded by pulling the plug out of his PC. Alex spent the rest of the weekend recovering critical data i.e. photos of Kylie Minogue in her underwear. Bella wondered if Alex would send an email to Kylie's website asking her to be an egg donor. She hoped Alex didn't think he actually got to shag an egg donor.

Bella knew she'd have to call the clinics from work and Alex had prepared a list for her. Dr Bunde had given them loads of information and she decided to read it on the way to work hidden within a copy of 'OK'. Bella quickly flicked through the leaflets until one caught her eye. It was advertising an infertility support group at the local hospital, meeting every first Monday of the month. Bella decided to call Alex, maybe they could go to this and check if any of these people had tried any of the local clinics or had any advice on Bella's egg problem.

"It's me, listen what are you doing tonight?"

"Nothing, why?"

"There's an infertility support group at the local hospital. I can't believe our luck. They meet on the first Monday of every month. We could go there tonight and find out if any other couples are in the same situation and if they've got any advice. We might even be able to find out about the different clinics we've short-listed."

"Sod that, is this some kind of joke?" Alex whispered. "If you think I am spending the evening with hormonal women drinking foul smelling tea you can forget it. I'd probably be the only bloke. Can you imagine it, hello my name's Alex and I've got issues with my sperm. No way Bella, no way."

"Do you have to be so negative, I really want to go."

"You can – on your own."

"I can't go on my own, what if it's all couples? Please Alex."

"No way, I draw the line at this. I'll go on the wagon, I'll take the disgusting vitamins, I'll go to every project roulette appointment but I will not go to some sodding support group…I know, take Jen."

"Jen, she's bloody pregnant, have you no tact? Taking a pregnant woman to an infertility support group, oh Alex please."

"Think about it she's not showing yet, you could get away with it. It's not like you're taking Maddie and Jake. Just tell her to keep it low key and for God's sake tell her not to throw up."

"I'll call her, but I am bloody angry you won't support me with this."

"Fine, you go with Jen and if you come back and say there were other blokes there, then I'm a prat, but if there aren't then clearly it's a bird thing and I'm off the hook."

Bella was furious. God help Alex if there were men there. Bella had to talk Jen into this. She quickly dialled her number.

"Hi, are you okay, it's me. I need a huge favour."

"I'm fine thanks, hang on let me stick the kids in front of the television."

"What can I do for you?"

"Could Guy babysit tonight?"

"He'll do anything for me this week. He came in totally trashed from the rugby and pissed in Jake's travel cot so he owes me big time. Why what's the occasion?"

"An infertility support group, Alex is refusing point blank to go and I really want to go. I want to talk to real people Jen, not just bloody doctors. This is so important to me."

"Shouldn't it be for couples? Won't we look like a couple of lesbians about to embark on a bit of turkey basting?"

"I'm not sure, if it is couples I'll just say my husband is away on business."

"Okay fine I'll do it."

"I can't thank you enough. I'll pick you up about seven, oh and try not to look pregnant."

"Why?"

"It's an infertility support group Jen, it just wouldn't look good."

"No problem, I've stopped throwing up now, honestly they'll never know."

Alex was not having a good day; Bella made him feel massively guilty about not going to this damn group thing. If there were any blokes there he'd pay for it big time. Bella called him to rub it in that Jen was going with her. Good old Jen and Guy, the poor sod, had to babysit as a result of something to do with Jake's travel cot.

His mobile interrupted Alex's guilt trip. It was Guy.

"Have you heard? Bella and Jen are off to an infertility support group tonight. Bella's apparently got the right hump because you won't go. I don't blame you mate. I bet they all wear flat shoes and hate men. I bet that's why half of them can't get pregnant because they frighten the sperm. You've done totally the right thing telling Bella to take Jen. Mind you what with Jen being pregnant, you couldn't get any one more fertile going to an infertility group. It's a bit like taking Kate Moss to weight watchers. Never mind, let them get on with it."

"Thanks mate, I knew you'd understand. Do me a favour as soon as Bella drops Jen off ask her if any blokes were there and text me. I need to be forewarned."

"Consider it done."

Bella was feeling nervous. They were late as usual and Jen felt sick, something to do with the smell of bleach in the hospital corridors. Jen apparently felt quite confident that with the aid of fizzy cola bottle sweets she could prevent any actual vomit. What a great start.

Bella took a deep breath and entered the room. It was packed. Everyone looked quite normal and there were no men, so Alex was off the hook. Bella quickly scanned the room. Surely not, it was only the assistant from hell, and what was she doing here?

"Oh my God Jen, we've got to go."

"Why, it looks alright to me. See that one over there who's troughing the biscuits, she's definitely pregnant, that makes me feel better anyway."

"You don't understand, one of my clients is here."

"No way, which one?"

"You know the one that's a total cow, Tamsin, the one that ruined our weekend in the Cotswolds by insisting I came back to London to sort out the problem she had caused by booking the wrong date for one of her artists. Anthony's always said he thought it was down to hormones. He could be right. What the hell am I going to do now?"

"Which one is she?"

"The one coming round with the leaflets, please don't tell me she's the organiser. That's it, we're leaving"

"She's seen you, she's coming over" whispered Jen.

Tamsin marched confidently over to Bella and Jen. "Well, normally I introduce myself and welcome new joiners. I'm the chairperson for the group. I guess we can skip the intros. Don't look so scared Bella. I'm only a total bitch at work. I set up this support group after our fifth failed cycle of IVF. We've stopped trying for a baby now. Once we stopped trying, I decided I could help couples going through infertility. I certainly have the experience! We normally chat for thirty minutes and I go and meet new joiners, then we have a guest speaker. This week, one of our members is coming in with her newly adopted baby to talk about the adoption process. Is there anything you feel the group can help you with? I take it's you that's looking for support not your friend who, please forgive me if I'm wrong, is pregnant "

Bella was lost for words. Tamsin was actually being pleasant, and so she was human after all.

"Yes it's me, we've just had some of the tests and I wanted to talk to real people not doctors and see if anyone had tried out any of the local clinics. We need to go straight to IVF."

"I think between us we've tried every clinic going and everyone's experience of each clinic is different. My only advice would be to check out the success rates they have for your age and condition if one has been diagnosed."

"That's really helpful. I think Alex was just looking at the overall success rates. The doctor seems to know what the problems are. Alex had a 'could do better' on his sperm count and my hormone levels aren't looking too great. Could be a problem with my egg quantity or quality, he doesn't really seem to know."

"You definitely need to check each clinic. Some have quite a strict protocol relating to fertility treatment and hormone levels. Sometimes if the levels aren't in the normal range they won't treat you. I know from experience, but my situation was more age related than yours. I was one of those having-it-all optimists who ignored the concept of fertility declining after 35. It's the last time I ignore the advice in the Daily Mail!"

"Oh Tamsin I'm so sorry, I really had no idea. Do you mean I could struggle to find a clinic that will do IVF for us?"

"No there are loads that will take you on, but some are a little more selective. You just need to call them and explain your situation. Look, I'll have to go. I need to introduce the guest speaker and don't worry I won't tell anyone at work. If you need any more help just buzz me on my mobile any time after work. Let me know how it's going."

Bella couldn't quite take it in, Tamsin was actually being sympathetic. Bella and Jen stayed and listened to the speaker who was talking so positively about accepting the fact she couldn't have her own biological children and her decision to adopt.

After the speaker had finished Bella and Jen left.

"I think we should go to these monthly Bella, you could get loads of information and support from people in the same situation. I'll book Guy in for babysitting. They didn't seem to have a problem with the fact I'm pregnant did they?"

"No, not at all, thanks Jen. I'm really pleased we went."

Bella dropped Jen off. Jen was quite surprised that Guy was so interested in the evening's events and attendees.

Alex was at home waiting for Bella. His phone beeped with a text message. Good old Guy, he'd got the low-down from Jen.

all birds, no blokes, flat shoes all round. just been booked in for babysitting. they are going every month. G.

Alex was relieved, at least he was off the hook. Alex heard Bella's car and went to greet her.

"How was it?"

"Great thanks and before you ask there weren't any men, although I was a little surprised to find one of my clients Tamsin was the chair person."

"No way, Anthony would love that, you bonding with a client at a 'can't get preggers' support group." He'd probably keel over. Did you learn anything?"

"Something quite major. We can't assume the list of clinics you have drawn up will treat us. Apparently some have guidelines on the hormone range they will treat within and I could be outside that."

"What do you mean, they select who they are going to treat even though we are paying? That's a good way of keeping their success rates high isn't it. Wish I could do the same on the trading desk."

"I don't know, we just need to call and ask. I'll do it tomorrow. I'm sure we'll find one. I do have age on my side unlike Tamsin"

"Yeah, she looks at least 50."

"She's not that old, she's probably about 42. Anyway she had five cycles of IVF so she must have found somewhere."

"Five cycles, wow, she must be well paid! What happened?"

"Don't know really, other than they have stopped trying for a baby. Please try and be more sensitive Alex. Look, I don't want to compare myself to Tamsin. Her situation could have been different. I'll call around tomorrow. Jen and I are going to go every month. Jen is just being brilliant, most of the girls know each other so it'll be great to take Jen. They seemed fine with the fact she's pregnant."

"Good, I'm pleased. I'll warn you, Guy thinks it's hilarious, like taking Kate Moss to weight watchers was the comparison he made."

"Well that's just charming of Guy. I don't care, it's great to have Jen there. I feel so much better, honestly, and I just really want to get going with the IVF now. I'll get onto it first thing."

Bella had secured a meeting room to call the clinics on their list. Why did she feel so nervous? It was like she was going to a job interview. She and Alex were paying for this, so shouldn't she be interviewing them?

Bella made all the calls. What she hadn't prepared herself for was waiting lists for appointments at some of the clinics. One of the clinics that Alex favoured seemed completely uninterested in even booking an appointment.

Bella decided to give the clinic Alex favoured another try. The clinic was quite close to her office and seemed to have really good success rates for IVF. Bella had a flashback to Jen's motivational speech. Surely this was like securing seat 1A or a room in a hotel that was full. She could and *would* get an appointment. After pleading with the frosty receptionist, who obviously was quite keen to get to lunch, an appointment was made for 48 hours later. It was hard to establish if this was the best clinic for them as all the clinics seemed hell bent on seeing them before providing success rates for their specific condition and age. Baby making seemed to be a very good business to be in. Bella arranged to have their notes faxed and she texted Alex with the appointment.

Chapter 12
Costly Exercise

Bella met Alex in the waiting room. Nothing could have quite prepared Bella for the experience of the waiting room. Whereas Dr Bunde's consulting room was in a major hospital and it felt like you were in a normal hospital, this was totally different and very odd.

Bella never felt the urge to leave a building in the same way as she did right now. The clinic was in an old building that was well presented but had this really sad feel to it. Bella remembered she and Alex once viewing a house where the owner had recently passed away and it felt really sad and empty. It was like the walls had absorbed all of the sadness and it was just hanging in the air. This is how this waiting room felt, sad, just so desperately sad.

It was busy. There were four other couples waiting. One couple brought their toddler with them who was busily drawing over one of the chintz sofas. Bella assumed they were trying to conceive number two but made a mental note to mention this to Guy next time he joked about the most fertile bird in Clapham attending an infertility support group. Bringing a baby to an IVF clinic, now that was pushing it.

One couple looked like they were attending a business meeting. They had three folders full of notes and looked like they were making a list of questions - obviously true IVF professionals. Bella could imagine them being on holiday and producing a windbreaker, Thermos flask and full picnic whilst she and Alex sat on a plastic hotel laundry bag arguing over whose idea it was not to bring the beach towels. The third couple were having a huge row, apparently something to do with the amount of time he had spent in the sample cupboard. The poor guy cowered whilst she berated him for not being able to produce a sample. The row was loud enough to distract Alex from the pictures of Kylie he was ogling in Bella's magazine.

The woman stormed out followed rather sheepishly by her husband.

"Bloody hell, poor guy. No wonder they're resorting to IVF. Can you imagine shagging her?"

"Shut up Alex."

Luckily Alex's commentary was interrupted by the appearance of a girl who rushed into the room clutching what could only be described as a paper hat. Immediately she threw up into it. Her husband looked rather shell-shocked.

"If you think I am ever damn well doing that again you're mistaken."

With that they left. Bella was wondering if she should be concerned. Her overriding desire to have a baby had given her little time to contemplate the physical stress of going through IVF. Would she be throwing up into a paper hat in a few weeks time?

"Mr Moore, please take this envelope to room five."

Alex was handed a brown envelope and a pot.

Oh my God, thought Bella, they're making him do a sample. Alex seemed to hold his pot aloft like he was toasting the potential success of his sperm test.

Bella kept looking at her watch and twenty minutes had passed. What the hell was he doing? She was just about to investigate when a rather stressed out Alex appeared clutching the brown envelope.

"Bloody weird place this is."

"Alex don't talk so loudly. What took you so long?"

"Don't you start. Have you ever tried to get aroused by an Argos catalogue?"

"What on earth are you talking about?"

"What I'm talking about Bella is the fact they didn't have any material in the sample room other than an Argos catalogue I found in the cupboard underneath the sink."

"So what did you do?"

"Looked at the lawnmowers."

"What?"

"Well, you know we were thinking of getting Mum one for Christmas now she can't afford to pay the gardener."

The nurse interrupted them.

"Excuse me, Mr Moore, could I ask that you return your brown envelope to reception please, patients aren't allowed to keep the magazines. Dr Williams is waiting for you in room five."

"Alex, really, didn't you look in the envelope?"

"Of course I didn't. It was sealed so I thought it contained our notes. What a stupid system."

Bella was amazed at Dr Williams' consulting room. It was a huge drawing room. Obviously it was a very lucrative profession, baby-making.

"Mr and Mrs Moore, please take a seat. I have reviewed your notes and I am waiting for your sperm results, Mr Moore, but it looks like it's straight to IVF. We just need to wait for a month considering Mrs Moore's hormone levels."

"Any questions?"

Bella could not believe this guy could charge £150 for a one-minute's conversation. No wonder the furniture was posh. Bella was determined to drag this out to get her money's worth.

"How do you know if it's a good month?"

"Quite simple. You need a blood test on day two of your period and we'll make an assessment. If your blood results indicate the right levels to respond to the drugs, we'll arrange for you to come in and collect the drugs and start treatment."

"You have my hormone levels in front of you. What if they get progressively worse?"

"They normally bounce around a bit. We just look for a good month."

"Okay, but Dr Bunde said he couldn't predict if I could or when I could enter an early menopause. What if I wait for a good month and miss the boat so to speak?"

"It's a risk we take, but there is really little point you having treatment unless your hormones are looking suitable for treatment."

Alex was starting to look agitated.

"What happens if they are not suitable for treatment, will IVF just not work?"

"Mr Moore, we do try and maximise your chances of success. We would not want you to waste your money."

"Okay, what if I said I don't want to risk my wife's results getting worse and I want us to start IVF on Bella's next cycle?"

"We would still test the hormone levels and would probably advise against treatment if they weren't at the correct levels."

"Dr Williams, I don't think you're hearing me. I am paying and I would like us to try a cycle of IVF next month, is that possible?"

"Of course it's possible but we might not recommend it."

"So what do you normally do with couples in our situation?"

"Wait for a good month."

"What if couples wait and there never is a good month?"

"We would review levels with them on an ongoing basis."

"What I guess I'm saying is are you prepared to offer your patients the choice or do you dictate who has treatment and when?"

"Mr Moore, you need to understand we are just trying to maximise your chances of success."

"What about your chances of success, Dr Williams? Aren't they measured by the percentage of successful cycles? Surely if you dictate when you are prepared to treat couples so there is a maximum chance of success, it would increase your clinic's performance?"

Oh my God thought Bella, Alex was going a bit too far.

"We are not in the habit of taking people's money when we know the likelihood is that the treatment won't work. Now if you'll excuse me, I'm just going to go to the lab to check your test results, Mr Moore."

"Alex, calm down."

"I am going to make this guy give us treatment whether he likes it or not, I'm paying. What if we do miss the boat Bella? I'll never forgive myself. Leave it to me, I'll close him down when he gets back."

"Alex, you're not on the trading desk now, what if he's right and it's a crap month I don't respond to the drugs and we waste thousands?"

"I don't care, at least we can look back and say we had a go. What if your hormones were never to improve, would we regret trying? I have a job at the moment so we can afford to take a gamble whilst I'm in work. Our situation may change Bella. We are doing IVF and doing it now and if Dr Pessimist won't do it, we'll find someone who will."

"Well you've certainly done a complete U-turn. Before it was 'oh let's leave it to nature, we've got time on our hands.'"

"Things have changed Bella. We clearly don't have time and I feel so guilty that I didn't take this thing more seriously. It's been you who has pushed me into going to the doctors. I just thought with you being 10 years younger the age thing would not be a problem. I know some older birds have problems, but not at your age. Bella I'm so sorry. I feel so bad and what if my sperm's still crap? That just makes the whole thing worse."

"I had no idea that you felt like this, it's not your fault. We've drifted along thinking time was on our side, we just need to deal with it. If you think it would be best for us to go ahead and you can bully Dr Williams into it, then let's just go for it. I don't ever want us to have any regrets."

Dr Williams reappeared.

"Mr Moore, I am delighted to say that your sperm does indicate that you are a suitable candidate for IVF. It has slightly improved since the last test."

"Right, well my wife and I have just had a chat and we want to go ahead with IVF irrespective of the results of my wife's blood tests, so could you just book us in please."

"Mrs Moore, please see the receptionist on your way out and she'll give you a form for a day 2 test. We will then arrange an appointment for you to have a scan and training on the drugs. I suggest you both attend the training so you can decide who will be administering the drugs. Reception is just down the hall on the right. Good luck."

Bella collected her form and they made a quick exit.

"Alex, I'm not sure about this. Dr Bunde at least made you feel like he wanted to help. You've just bullied this guy into giving us IVF. Is he really going to give it his all or has he already written us off?"

"Look, Bella, it's not like you're going to be treated because you're ill. I am quickly learning that this is big business. He is going to do the treatment and why would it be in his interests to knowingly let us fail? He has success rates that he doesn't want to impact. Do I like him? No. Am I pissed off that we just paid £150 for what was in effect a 10-minute consultation? Yes. Do I honestly know the best way forward? No. What I do know is if we leave it we face the risk of your hormone levels becoming worse. If we have a go and fail at least we can always look back and say we tried."

"Okay, it's just such a lot of money Alex, and he was suggesting that if the levels aren't right the treatment won't work. It looks like he is just going to allow us to pursue what he considers to be a mad folly."

"Let's just see what your levels are like next week and take it from there. Whilst I'm still hanging onto my job we can afford to take a risk. I have to get back to work. I'll call you later"

Alex quickly kissed Bella and raced off towards the tube. Bella spent the rest of the afternoon dipping in and out of the Internet looking up hormone levels, as work was luckily fairly quiet. Bella couldn't quite believe how common this problem seemed to be. There were chat rooms full of women comparing blood test results and discussing which drugs had worked, along with numerous emotionally fraught descriptions of failed treatment. Bella wished she'd done more research. Alex was right. They had left it two years. Maybe if they went to the doctors earlier things would have been different? How could she blame Alex? They agreed to leave it to nature. He always told her not to worry as she had age on her side, what a joke.

Bella's phone buzzed. "Bella it's Tamsin. Rick's not happy. He doesn't like the hotel you booked in New York; in fact he hates it. I'll forward you his voicemail. I suggest you move him now before he totally loses it. He's really pissed off. He has even thrown some of the complimentary bath products at the maid. Honestly, Bella, I don't need this. Can you just make sure you never ever put him in there again."

"Sure, are there any hotels in New York he does like? I just can't seem to recall any. We've moved him at least three times on every trip"

"Don't ask me, that's your job. Go through all his files and book somewhere he hasn't stayed before."

"Okay fine, I'll get straight onto it."

"Did you get a clinic? Are you okay to talk about it now?"

"I did get a clinic, but I feel awkward talking to you about it at work. Can I just get on with the New York hotel?"

"Sure, if you fancy a quick drink after work, you can tell me all about it if you want."

"Actually, Tamsin, I'd really like that, as I am really worried about it."

"Okay, I'll see you in Trepido at 6 p.m."

"Great, thanks. I'll email you with Ricky's hotel."

"Just don't piss him off again Bella, see you at 6."

It took the rest of the day to find a hotel in New York that Ricky hadn't stayed in. Bella finally found a new boutique style property that she hoped Tamsin could convince him was very trendy so he felt he had to like it. She quickly emailed Tamsin and headed off to the wine bar. Bella was struggling with this new relationship with Tamsin. One minute Tamsin was screaming at her, and the next minute they were having a cosy glass of wine discussing egg reserves. God, this was weird.

Tamsin was late as usual. Bella decided to grab a quick glass of wine. She hadn't had a drink since Jen and Guy's supper, but felt she needed one tonight. While she was queuing, she quickly sent a text to Alex to let him know she was having an after work fertility pow wow with Tamsin.

Tamsin made her grand entrance and did a few dramatic air kisses.

"Thanks for sorting that tosser's hotel darling. He's on his way to it now. I've told him it is absolutely the place to be seen at right now, so I'm sure he'll be fine."

"No problem. I've also had his mini-bar stocked with his favourite champagne so hopefully he won't notice the size of the awfully trendy cupboard he is staying in,"

Tamsin laughed.

"So what's happened with the clinic?"

"Well, Alex wants to go to a clinic with higher success rates than those of Dr Bunde, so we went to a private one today. It was bloody awful to be honest. Alex had to bully the doctor into treating us because of my hormone levels. It was like Alex was at work trying to close a deal. I never realised it was like this."

"I guess they gave you the piece about it not working if the levels aren't right, blah blah blah."

"Totally, but what are you supposed to do Tamsin, how do you know which way it's going to go? Anyway we've decided to go ahead and I'm going to have my blood test next week."

"I've done both Bella, with my first cycle I just went for it and actually responded fairly well - three eggs I think, but I failed to get pregnant. After that I tried to go for a good month but the results varied. I had one really good month with my levels and was confident and they did get eight eggs but only one fertilised and I didn't become pregnant. Mind you, as they kept saying to me, it only takes one egg. I was just unlucky and Bella, please remember that I am considerably older than you. If you produce eggs at your age they are probably of a better quality so I would imagine you stand a much better chance. For every story like mine there are a hundred successful ones. There's no right and wrong, just see how your levels are next week and take it from there."

"Sorry Tamsin, I can't believe I'm asking you this, but how did you cope with all the failed cycles and ultimately a child free life? Sorry to be so personal but you do seem very together about it."

"I am now, but going through IVF is emotionally and physically draining and it took its toll on me. I felt in the end that I had no quality of life. It caused huge problems in my relationship. I don't know if you're aware but Rod left me two years ago and I was devastated. So I decided to get my life back on track and to do that I needed to stop trying for a baby and accept that I could have a happy and fulfilled life without children."

"God, Tamsin, that must have been hard."

"Yes, it was considering Rod had meet someone 15 years younger and she fell pregnant within six months."

"Bloody hell."

"Well it didn't work out and before the baby was born, Rod and I got back together and we are so happy. He says we've got our life back and I agree. Me being a mother just wasn't meant to be. I'm now quite friendly with his ex-girlfriend and his daughter stays with us every weekend. Although I could never imagine myself in this position, I'm actually really happy. I just think it wasn't meant to be."

"You've done so well. I just can't see that I'd ever be able to contemplate a life without children."

"You don't need to right now. Just focus on the treatment Bella, don't go into this thinking you might not be able to have children. Be positive, don't anticipate failure."

"I know you're right. Thanks so much for the chat Tamsin. Just as an aside are IVF clinics normally so bloody depressing?"

"Just wait 'til the husbands start comparing how many eggs their wives have produced. It's hideous. At least you'll be one of the youngest. I remember being late for my egg retrieval. I think I'd only got about three eggs and I spent 40 minutes doing my make up so it didn't look like I was past it. Rod was completely baffled as to why I'd got my full evening slap on under general anaesthetic. I told him to shut up or fund Botox. Let me know how it goes, won't you? Just buzz me on the mobile."

"Thanks, Tamsin."

Bella felt a bit better. Tamsin was right. No point in worrying about failure. She just needed to give it her best shot. Bring on Bella vs. Infertility, Round 1.

Chapter 13
Round 1

Bella went for her blood test as planned and her hormone levels were only marginally worse. Bella and Alex were sat in the waiting room in anticipation of being scanned and trained on the injections.

Bella was feeling nervous. The receptionist already told her that Dr Williams said the results were not suitable for IVF. But as Alex said earlier, although they were only marginally worse they still hadn't got better so he was still adamant that they go for it. She couldn't believe they were about to embark on something so major that for them only had about a 5% success rate, i.e. it had 95% chance of failing. What the bloody hell were they doing?

Bella was dreading telling Anthony. She needed to find out how much time she would need to take off work. If she could scan at 8 a.m. and take a day's holiday for the egg retrieval, she might get away with it.

The snotty receptionist called them through.

Dr Williams rushed into his consulting room in his full surgical gear.

"Mr & Mrs Moore, sorry I'm late. An egg retrieval took longer than planned. Okay, I've looked at your results Mrs Moore, and as you know they are slightly worse than last month. Nothing major but they are slightly worse. As you know my advice is not to go ahead but I understand from my receptionist that you are both determined to do IVF this month."

Alex was starting to get annoyed.

"Hang on a minute, we are not determined as in totally bloody-minded. We are determined to try a cycle of IVF because we're both worried that Bella's results could actually get worse. Seemingly, neither you nor Dr Bunde is able to guarantee that they aren't going to, so on that basis we are going ahead. Please don't make it sound like we are just hell bent on having a cycle of IVF. I would not put my wife through this if I felt we had any real choice."

"I have not said that I'm not prepared to treat you. I just want to manage your expectations and as there is considerable money involved, I want you to be aware that it is unlikely to be successful."

"Well, we are perfectly aware, so can we just get on with it please?"

Dr Williams spent the next five minutes scanning Bella behind a screen and declared everything was fine. Bella didn't like the prospect of a gowned man whom Alex had just shouted at brandishing a condom covered probe. He then handed them over to the nurse who took them through sniffing and shooting up as Alex put it. Bella was placed on something called a short protocol and was due to start sniffing at 7 p.m. They would start the injections in a couple of days. Alex received his training on injections for which they had opted to use the gun on the basis that needles made Alex nervous. Bella had a chat with the receptionist and as the clinic opened at 7 a.m. she reckoned she could get away without telling Anthony.

They walked to the tube holding hands.

"How you feeling, Bella?"

"Great considering that miserable bastard has just told me in not so many words that it's going to fail and I'm carrying nearly two grand's worth of drugs in a bloody carrier bag on the tube."

"Ignore him, as that Tamsin bird said it only takes one egg and this could be the month."

"I know. I'll start the nose spray thing tonight. I guess we'll just have to take it one step at a time."

When Bella was off the tube she called Jen.

"Hi it's me, can you talk?"

"Yes, they're round next door. I'm waiting for the video repairman. Jake's fed the video biscuits again. Fran's agreed to have them for half an hour. Remember last time he was here, Jake inadvertently poked him with a screwdriver, very nasty. Have you been to the clinic?"

"Yes, I'm just on my way back to work, managed to fit it into my lunch hour. My results are slightly worse. I think Alex is worried they're on a downwards cycle so we're going ahead with the treatment. I start sniffing the nose spray tonight and Alex has this gun thing to do the injections. I start those in a few days."

"Do you need to tell work? What about your parents, do they know?"

"No to both. I think I can fit it in around work. We talked about telling my parents and Alex's mum but I can't face a cast of thousands tracking my follicles. You can just imagine my mother at the butchers discussing ovarian stimulation – no thanks. It's just you and Guy for now."

"Okay, the video bloke is here, call me and let me know how the drugs are going. We're keeping everything crossed."

"I will, thanks Jen."

Bella started the nasal spray. They didn't tell you about the almighty head rush you got in the side effects list. Everything she ate afterwards tasted more toxic than usual. After a couple of days, Bella went for a scan and they started the injections. Bella called Alex to make sure he would be home from work on time. They decided to do them in the evenings as in theory they would be less rushed.

Bella didn't feel great. After each spray she was getting headaches and felt irritable. She hadn't eaten much of her dinner and noticed Alex had barely touched his.

"Right girl, it's time to shoot up. Upstairs we go and for God's sake keep Ginger out. Knowing him, he'll leap up at the wrong time and I'll end up injecting him."

Bella watched Alex prepare and mix the drugs. He must have washed his hands at least ten times, and she noticed he was shaking.

He was hovering over her thigh with the injection gun.

"Alex, I don't need the suspense just put it in…. aaargghh bloody hell!"

"Did it hurt darling?"

"No it was fine."

"Liar, listen to Ginger, he's howling on the landing, probably thinks I've killed you."

"You nearly bloody did," hissed Bella under her breath. "It's okay it just feels like I've been punched in the leg. I'm sure it's just the force of the gun that's all. I'm going to bed, I don't feel so good."

Bella and Alex carried on with the sniffing and shooting for 7 days until it was time to have the scan. Alex arranged to accompany Bella and secured a 7 a.m. appointment.

Bella was really nervous. She assumed they'd find out if she had responded to the drugs. She decided to invite Alex to sit on her side of the screen on the understanding that he didn't laugh at the huge condom covered probe.

Dr Williams was poking around for ages and finally he showed them one black blob.

"There is only one follicle. We would consider this to be a poor response. We'll scan you again in a couple of days to re-check and see how it's going, but you may want to consider if things don't improve either abandoning the cycle or converting it to IUI if the follicle reaches a good size. I'll need you to have another blood test, Bella, so we can review your levels."

Was it Bella's imagination or was Dr Williams looking particularly pleased with his ability to predict failure? Bella hoped it wouldn't come to this. She quickly pulled up her knickers and they went back to the waiting room.

"Please stay with me while I have my blood test Alex. I feel too numb to function at the moment."

"Don't panic Bella, the old git's probe is probably not working properly and everything's okay. Even if there's only one follicle like he said, we can go for IUI. The game isn't over yet."

"It feels like it is Alex. I think we need to look into egg donation."

"Bella just calm down. We're nowhere near that point."

"I can't calm down, I feel totally bloody mental. I don't know if it's these sodding drugs that drag you down but I feel like it is game over. This isn't just about failure; it's a bloody disaster. I'm not going to even get as far as having my eggs retrieved, let alone bleeding fertilised."

Bella could hear three women comparing the numbers of follicles they had so cleverly managed to produce.

"If they don't shut up I swear I'll have that 15 follicle bird by the throat in a minute."

Alex looked very panicky.

"It must be the drugs talking. I've never seen you so fiery. It could be quite attractive really but not right now, just calm down."

Bella had never been in such a bad mood. She felt awful, and she could barely speak to the woman taking her blood.

"Right, I'm back off to work now, just to be told I've upset about ten different clients because nothing I do is right, let's face it."

"Bella, I think you should go home."

"No way, I'll just get on with it. That's what everyone expects isn't it? Good old Bella just gets on with it. I'm taking this cab, I'll see you later."

Bella's mobile rang. It was Jen. Bella briefly told her about her egg debacle and promised she'd call her later in the week. Bella was starting to feel relieved. She hadn't told anybody else. She could just imagine her mother calling an emergency coffee morning to discuss her one sodding miserable follicle.

Bella and Alex went back for the next scan, and there it sat, the lonely follicle, although Dr Williams assured them it was a good size and booked them in for turkey basting on Sunday. Apparently IVF was not an option, as Dr Williams didn't feel it was appropriate given the fact they hadn't a hope in hell or, as he put it, the poor response meant they were not suitable candidates for IVF. Even Alex had accepted this as he seemed to have in his head that one egg would be fine anyway and they could conceive via IUI now his sperm had picked up.

If it wasn't for the mind-bending drugs, Bella could have written this off as a practice run and reconcile the failure. However, emotions were getting the better of her and she was secretly hoping Alex was right. If he was, they wouldn't even have to go through the IVF bit, how wonderful. On top of all this, it was the monthly Guy, Jen, Andrew and Susannah supper on Friday, two nights before basting. Predictably, Guy and Jen were hosting due to the national shortage of willing and able babysitters. To add to the nightmare they just discovered that Alex needed to give Bella a final injection on the monthly supper night and Alex had told Bella they'd discuss it later. Bella had already decided they were going. She was not prepared to put their life on hold for this crap, look what happened to Tamsin.

She was pretty sure she could blag it that she was embarking on a detox, to explain the no drinking and violent mood swings, and Alex could pretend he was completely hung-over from the night before so had decided to drive and not drink. Perfect, she'd brief Jen. Also, by the time the clock struck midnight, she was sure Guy and Andrew would be too pissed to notice them sneak upstairs for a quick shot of drugs. Perfect.

Chapter 14
Pop Socks and Syringes

Bella felt awful and knew she looked hideous. Her stomach was bloated and her hair was limp and dull. She decided to wear an old pair of white linen drawstring trousers on the basis they wouldn't cut her in half and would allow fast access to shoot up at midnight. So what if it was the middle of February, she was too hormonal to care.

Jen briefed Guy and asked him not to get too drunk in case of a medical emergency.

Why did Bella feel nervous sitting in Jen's kitchen waiting for the arrival of the pregnant princess? Maybe it was the ongoing head rush she was experiencing that was slightly tipping her over the edge. Bella sighed as she heard them arrive. Here we go again, she thought.

"Bella darrrrling," drawled Susannah. "My God aren't you cold? There's a ground frost out there."

Nothing compared to the big chill in here thought Bella, stupid cow.

"Well Susannah I'm on a big detox, so sweating like mad, wouldn't sit too close if I were you. How are you, have you stopped throwing up? "

"I'm feeling fantastic now thank you."

Andrew put a loving arm around her.

"She's just glowing isn't she, you know everything they say about pregnant women being sexy, well it's totally true."

"You should try it you know."

"What, looking sexy?"

"No, getting pregnant. No disrespect but you and Alex look like you've been partying hard again."

"No only Alex has darling, Bella's on a detox."

"Really, remind me not to buy that book."

Bella was just not in the mood.

The boys went into the lounge for their pre-dinner drinks, leaving Bella with the pregnant princess and a rather harassed Jen who was desperately trying to cook a meal in the midst of the increasing tension at the kitchen table.

"I've found a fab maternity boutique Jen. I've decided to opt for outfits that promote whilst flatter my bump. You have to be so careful at our stage in pregnancy Jen. I just wouldn't want people to think I was fat. I'll drop a catalogue round if you like."

"Don't worry, I tend to buy jogging bottoms from Asda, normally two sizes bigger, plus some of Guy's old tops. I have some smart stuff from when I was pregnant with Maddie, but I can't really fit into that any more. You can borrow some of that stuff if you want."

"Save it for Bella. I really have more than I need. Anyway, Bella, isn't it about time you and Alex thought about starting a family? I know you still like to take the free travel with your job but you can still have children and travel. Having a family doesn't need to change your life. You can get them to fit around the lifestyle you want. That's what Andrew and I intend to do."

Jen was making strange choking noises at the cooker.

"And there's the age factor Bella, just don't risk it, not everyone is as lucky as Andrew and I. I feel sorry for these career women who don't start trying until their late thirties. It's really sad that they could remain childless. Mind you no less than they deserve. There's no excuse these days. You only have to pick up a newspaper to read about declining fertility rates."

"Susannah would you mind rounding the boys up please, I'm about to serve."

Jen put her arm protectively around Bella.

"Ignore the stupid cow, she hasn't got a clue."

"She's got a point Jen, but the thing is I'm not one of these try-to-have-it-all career women. I started trying two years ago and I certainly haven't got a career to speak of."

"Just ignore her, what time are you shooting up?"

"Midnight. Alex is really nervous as we can't do this one in the gun, so he's got to play doctor tonight, that's why he is totally banned from alcohol."

"Well all the best, we'll distract the pregnant princess and don't worry, Andrew will be too pissed to notice."

Bella could not focus on the rest of the meal. Andrew and Guy were drunk and arguing about a rugby match they played when they were thirteen. Alex spent most of the night looking at his watch and pushing his food around the plate.

Bella agreed with Alex that she would fake illness at 11:30 and go for a lie down. Alex would then check on her at 11:50 and quickly administer the injection.

All was going to plan. No one questioned Bella's illness. She knew she looked awful anyway, so she didn't even have to rely on her previous amateur dramatic experience.

She lay down and waited for her medic in shining armour to appear. On cue, Alex arrived looking very pale.

"How are you feeling darling?"

"Alex, no need to shout, you'll wake the kids. They can't hear you downstairs now that Guy's put that awful music on."

"Hey, be a good wifey and don't knock the power of Led Zeppelin," said Alex as he read the instruction leaflet about ten times. "This is bloody ridiculous, should people really be doing this sort of thing at home without proper supervision?"

"Just do it Alex."

"OK, I'm ready, take a deep breath darling... aaarrrgghhhh. Bloody Hell, I've stuck it in my sodding thumb."

"What on earth are you two up to in here?" asked Andrew as he entered the room.

Oh no, thought Bella, not Andrew. She took a mental picture of the scene. Alex was trying to stop his thumb bleeding over Jen's duvet whilst balancing a syringe in his other hand. Bella then looked at herself. She had taken her white linen trousers off to avoid bloodstains and had huge pants on and, oh my God, pop socks on. She only just realised she hadn't taken them off after work. Andrew looked visibly shocked. Bella couldn't work out if it was the pop socks or the syringe that had done it.

"It's not how it looks Andrew, we're not doing drugs or anything. Bella's got this illness."

Bella was so stressed she could barely speak. Why didn't Andrew just piss off out of the room rather than staring childlike at her crumpled pop socks?

"Ignore him Andrew, we're having fertility treatment and if you don't leave the room now and let Alex do this injection you may cost Alex thousands. He's trying to release my eggs by injecting me in the stomach and we'd prefer it if we could continue our romantic moment in private – thanks."

"And as for you Alex, don't even open your bloody mouth, just stick the injection in my stomach now."

Andrew mumbled something and backed out of the room.

"That's it, don't worry about me. What if some of that stuff has got into my bloodstream? I think we should call a doctor, this could be serious."

"Stick the needle in my stomach now Alex."

Great, they were 10 minutes late. Bella hoped it hadn't messed up the timing of the egg release. It wasn't like she had a few to spare.

"It's in, there we go. Did that hurt?"

"Far less than the gun actually. Oh my God Alex, I can just imagine the smug 'baby on board' brigade downstairs doing a post-mortem on 'Barren Bella'."

"Believe me, Andrew will be convinced my sperm are malfunctioning. He'll probably be quite pleased it's another thing he can add to his list that he can do better."

"Let's get out of here. I'm feeling rough and if the pregnant princess talks once more about women who have left it too late to become preggers, I swear I'll have her hanging from the ceiling by her maternity pashmina. I don't want to offend Guy and Jen. Could you just tell them I'm not feeling well and I'll wait in the car?"

Bella fumbled her way downstairs and outside to the car. Her head was swimming and she was so damn hot. She saw a rather flustered Alex stumble out the front door.

"How did you manage to get out so quickly?

"Simple, I just went into the kitchen and said, sorry you all had to find out about our inability to conceive a baby without medical intervention through Bella being caught with her trousers down and me stabbing myself with a needle. We have to leave now as Bella could be laying eggs in the car as we speak. Hope you understand and wish us luck with the stirrups and turkey baster on Sunday. Bye."

"I love you."

"I thought you'd be really mad."

"Not at all. I couldn't have put it better myself. Anyway like you said, it might only take one egg and we could be smug 'baby on boards' in a couple of weeks."

"Yes and hopefully it will be the last time the Tesco's van has to deliver a pregnancy test, tampons and gin.

Chapter 15
Pirates, Princesses and a Dalek

'It only takes one egg' seemed great in theory but Bella's period pains were telling her otherwise.

Why had she let Anthony talk her into helping him out at yet another meeting? She could not believe she was sitting in another death-by-PowerPoint presentation in the middle of what could be the opening act of a life without children.

Bella managed to do six have-I-failed-to-conceive knicker checks that morning, including two in the lift. Bella needed to do a final check right now, just to confirm the failure, but this month it wasn't just an average failure, oh no, this month they had paid thousands so it was an expensive failure. At least the smug git at the clinic would be pleased.

Bella looked around the room. Everyone was bored to tears. Anthony had been talking for over an hour. Bella had to check her knickers and she was toying with sticking her fingers down her tights under the table to liven up the proceedings, but decided to fake a quick coughing fit and retreat to the ladies. She could have sworn Tamsin knew what she was up to.

At least the toilets were empty.

Bella stood in the cubicle for ages.

"Please, God, let me be pregnant. I'll never say another bad word about smug 'baby on board' people. Please God help me."

Bella did the seventh knicker check. Out flowed the sea of red.

"Oh please God no" Bella dropped to her knees sobbing.

Bella quickly dialled Alex.

"It's me, can you talk?"

"Not really a good time, what's up?"

"Best get online to Tesco's."

"Oh my God Bella, do you need to do a test?"

"No Alex, I just need the gin and tampons. I just got my period."

"How are you feeling?"

"I don't know, angry actually, angry that the git at the clinic was right, angry that I'm stuck in one of Anthony's presentations and angry that I've failed so spectacularly. I think if I had got as far as IVF with a few eggs to spare then at least I would know we were just maybe unlucky this time. What am I to think now? Alex, we really need to start looking at egg donation."

"Bella calm down, I think you should go home and I'll try and leave early."

"I can't, Anthony will go mad. They're just about to have a Q&A session and you know what he's like, he doesn't do Q's let alone A's. To be honest Alex, it's a relief. At least I know and haven't got to keep checking my knickers every 10 minutes. I'd rather be busy than sit at home miserable."

"Okay if that's what you want, call me later and Bella I really am sorry it didn't work out for us this time, but it's only the first attempt and the success rates for this are lower than, er, project roulette. We'll get there. We just need to talk about where we go from here."

"Yeah Dr Barnados," Bella mumbled.

"Dr who, is he supposed to be good?"

"Don't worry Alex I'll call you later."

Bella managed to get through the rest of the presentation and completely immersed herself in work for the rest of the day. It was easier to cope with complete and utter failure if you didn't have time to think about it.

Bella knew Jen would be anxious to know and decided to call round on her way back from work.

Bella instantly regretted the decision when she entered the house in the middle of a pirates and princesses tea party in aid of Children In Need. It was total mayhem.

Bella eventually managed to locate Jen who was trying to control a jelly fight between a vicious looking pirate and a dalek. Jen explained that the mother of the dalek works full time and hadn't time to get him a pirate's outfit.

Jen outsourced the jelly fight management to the neighbour's au pair and ushered Bella upstairs.

"Look Jen, I'll just go. This clearly isn't a good time, I should have phoned."

"Your timing couldn't be better. If the mother of dalek child does not get back from work in the next thirty minutes, I will not be responsible for my actions. I need a breather, so how's it going?"

"It's gone Jen, my one lonely follicle has failed to produce so we've failed. Bella vs. Infertility Round 1, Bella 0 - Infertility 1"

"Oh Bella, I'm so sorry. How you feeling?"

"Scared, really scared. I can't really explain it but I think if we got as far as IVF and had a really good crack at the treatment, I'd have felt that we had a fighting chance, but we didn't even get as far as IVF. I don't know where we go from here. I called the clinic earlier as you have to report the outcome. They didn't give a damn. Apparently the next appointment they have available to discuss my failed cycle is in three months. I slammed the phone down. If Alex thinks I'm ever going back to that place with Dr Doom, there is no way. If we ever do this again, Jen, I need to find another clinic. I'm never walking back through those doors again."

"I'm sure there are better clinics. It's the infertility group meeting tomorrow. Let's go and find out about other clinics. I'm sure there will be better ones."

"Thanks Jen, I'd like that. I'd also like to talk to them about egg donation. There are clinics where you can go on waiting lists for donor eggs. I would imagine it takes a long time to get a match but if I'm running out of eggs it might be my only chance."

"There was an article in the paper recently about the removal of donor anonymity. They reckon it could reduce supply even further."

"Alex looked on some USA websites where you can pay for donors. You should see the costs Jen. If you're blonde, blue-eyed and Ivy League you can earn thousands. I think Alex was going to send the link to Guy, as there were some real "babes" apparently. Alex is reluctant to go down that route, but anyway we would need counselling first. He keeps saying it's too early to even discuss it, but if it takes years to get a donor, I think we may as well get on the list."

"How do you feel about the baby being biologically Alex's and not yours?"

"I don't know, I would need to think it all through, but right now I do see it as an option. I'll let you get back to the pirates, princesses and dalek party. Sorry I called round at such a crap time."

"You haven't. If you can bear to be around children today, feel free to stay for a glass of wine. One encounter with dalek brat and you may never want to visit an IVF clinic again. Buzz Alex if you want and he can pop in. But if you prefer to stay on your own tonight, I'll understand."

"Actually, I don't want to be on my own, that would be great. I can help you clear up and Alex can call in for me on his way back from work."

When Alex eventually arrived stinking of beer, Bella was too squiffy to even notice. Whilst helping Jen clear up the aftermath, she'd manage to plough her way through a bottle of wine. Guy had already texted Jen from behind a bush in the front garden to see if all the kids had departed.

Jen decided that Bella and Alex needed to be fed and looked after as they were both clearly too far gone to do anything other than grab a kebab. Bella had decided to stop drinking wine and was mopping up the alcohol by gratefully tucking into one of Jen's homemade casseroles. Jen and Guy were bathing Maddie and Jake.

Alex was looking really rough.

"I've had a crap day. Firstly the news about the treatment, and secondly a deal's gone belly up at work. If they blame me for this one it could be game over."

"Alex, we can't afford for you to lose your job now. We'll never be able to afford egg donation on my salary."

"Whoa slow down, who said anything about egg donation? Plus I'll find another job if I need to so we can afford the treatment."

"Was it your fault?"

"It never has anything to do with whose fault it is, just who they are going to make as a scapegoat. As it happens whilst I've been involved, it's not directly my fault but as my results are fairly crap compared to everyone else's, you can bet it'll me down to me. Let's face it, Dominic won't take the blame for anything. He'll come out of it as the blue-eyed boy. He'll set someone else up as the fall guy. That's the way he's always survived in the City - by being a total bastard."

"Great Alex, just what we need."

"Don't worry about it for now. I'm surprised you came round here especially in the middle of a kid's party."

"Look, Alex, I'm fine around kids and I didn't want to be on my own. I had a good chat with Jen and you don't know this yet, but having been told by Dr Doom's receptionist that they can't discuss our failure for another 3 months, I want us to look at other clinics. Jen's offered to come with me to the infertility group again tomorrow night and we're going to look into other options. I do want us to seriously look into egg donation Alex."

"Bella you're just panicking. I agree we need to change clinics, but egg donation - that's a big step Bella and we've only just had one failed cycle."

"It could take years to get a suitable donor. I just want to research it Alex, that's all."

"Okay darling let's just look into it for now. Maybe one of the barren brigade can recommend a clinic."

"For God's sake Alex don't call them that. I'm finding it really helpful to know there is a support group I can go to and Tamsin's been great. I know it's not your thing but Jen's really happy to go with me and Jen is being fantastic. You know she's normally quite matter of fact. You remember the first conversation I had with her on the phone after you'd told Guy? Well, she is being really supportive. I guess she must find it hard with them having kids so easily."

"She's an old trooper Jen is, always has been, there for anyone when the chips are down. She's not one to wear her heart on her sleeve you know."

"What has Guy said?"

"He's really sad for us. I think he finds it hard to say the right thing you know. I tried to talk to him about it in the bush outside but it was hard to hear his response as a small child was shouting 'exterminate' in a rasping voice. Shall we make a move? I need to be in early tomorrow, so I can monitor the movements to and from Dominic's office. I know the signs, if the bird from HR appears followed by the post room guy with a brown box, I reckon I'll be the one."

"A brown box?"

"Yeah, they have the contents of your desk packed whilst they get you to sign a compromise agreement."

"Great, that place is bloody barbaric Alex."

"I know. I wouldn't mind but they used to have a taxi waiting for you. We always used to know if there was going to be a mass clear out due to the number of black cabs outside. Now what with all the cutbacks, they don't even give you the bloody bus fare. Anyway you know what they're like. I just hope I manage to ride this storm."

Bella and Alex said goodbye to Jen and Guy and decided to have an early night. Alex needed to survive another brown box exit tomorrow and Bella needed to get into work on time to get everything done in time to make it to the support group.

Chapter 16
Round 2

Alex texted Bella to let her know that he survived another day. Dominic made it clear that Alex would be next and he couldn't protect his sorry arse any longer. Bella was amazed Alex had managed to last this long. He actually hated it and seemed only able to survive through his network of old mates of which surprisingly Dominic was one.

Bella received a coded email from Tamsin enquiring if she was going to attend the group. Bella confirmed and checked if it was okay for the ever-growing Jen to come along. Apparently a woman was going to be giving a talk on her successful treatment and bringing along her twins. Tamsin asked if Jen could help out with them whilst the woman did her presentation. Bella emailed to say she thought Jen would be honoured. She was sure Jen would actually be pissed off as the infertility group meetings seemed to be her only child-free event of the month.

They arrived at the hospital only 10 minutes late. Tamsin came rushing over with the twins.

"Darlings, so glad you could make it. Cassie's just about to start. It's so good of you Jen to look after Henry and

Benjamin while she talks to the group. Poor girl hasn't slept for weeks but she's determined to do her bit."

Jen glared at Bella as both twins screamed in unison.

Jen popped the twins into a double buggy and was doing laps of the meeting room while Cassie gave her view on how IVF can be a positive experience. Bella guessed in comparison to the screaming two, it probably was.

Cassie could not speak highly enough of the clinic they went to and bearing in mind she changed clinics three times, Bella figured she'd have a pretty good idea. Bella decided to ask her during herbal tea and flapjacks.

Jen resorted to carrying both babies around in turns, "something to do with colic" Jen muttered to Bella on her seventh circuit with Henry.

"Your friend Jen is just fabulous with the twins Bella."

"Yes, she's got two of her own and number three is on its way. Jen's pretty experienced. I really enjoyed your talk Cassie. Your experience with your last clinic seemed so positive. Do you think that was because you had successful treatment there?"

"No, I had two failed cycles there, but they always made me feel fine about it. They were always so caring and reassuring that we would get a positive result."

"Do you mind me asking which one you used? I'm finding that some aren't interested in treating me because of my hormone levels."

"Redwoods is where I went to. They take on loads of difficult cases. They aren't bothered about the impact to success rates. They just seem to want to help. Some say they just want your money by taking on cases other hospitals have deemed hopeless, but I didn't see it that way. They were the first people who made me feel like I had a fighting chance. Call them and explain your situation."

"Do they do egg donation?"

"Absolutely, we went on the list when we started our first cycle. Fortunately, we conceived on our third attempt there but it was good to know we had a back up plan. I'm 42, so I didn't want to wait too long. Look I'd better go, they're due a feed."

"Thanks so much. I'll call them tomorrow.

Poor Jen looked knackered.

"Jen, thanks for helping out. Guess what, I may have just found another clinic.

"Fantastic, can we go home now. I need a lie down."

Alex was a bit happier having survived another week at work, so Bella decided to crack on with the new clinic while the going was good.

It seemed like fate was working in their favour. Luckily a couple had cancelled their appointment for the following day and a doctor who was actually writing a medical paper about hormone responses to fertility drugs was available and very keen to meet with them.

Bella was excited and called Alex to give him the good news.

Bella could not believe his response.

"I can't do 11 a.m. Dominic is breathing down my neck, can the guy not do 8 a.m.?"

"Alex, we've managed to get a cancellation. We don't know how much time we've got on our side. You'll have to tell Dominic that you've got a doctor's appointment."

"If I do, it won't just be my desk contents that will be in a brown box Bella."

"I'm not arguing about this Alex, just tell him."

"Fine, but don't blame me if he fires me."

"Of course not Alex, you're never to blame for anything."

Redwoods could not have been any more different to the previous clinic from hell. Firstly, it was in a proper hospital and was painted pink and felt really inviting, almost womb-like.

The receptionists were friendly and courteous and there were a few waiting rooms so couples weren't thrown in together. There was a TV and some trashy magazines to add to the warm glow. Instantly Bella relaxed. Luckily, Alex didn't have to produce a sample as they were using the results from the previous test. After Bella's telephone battle with Miss Frosty pants at the previous clinic, she managed to have all their notes faxed to Tamsin's private fax machine. Anthony would kill Bella if he knew they had been comparing Alex's sperm to Rod's over a cup of herbal tea.

The consultation lasted for over an hour whilst the consultant explained various ways of altering the drugs protocol to see if Bella would respond better to another way of managing the treatment. Bella was impressed. In essence it could have been the drugs that failed her not the other way round. This was looking promising. He seemed quite keen to start another cycle in a few months time irrespective of her hormone levels.

All was going well until they got onto the subject of egg donation. The consultant recommended that they go on the waiting list at a cost of £150. It all sounded very sensible to Bella.

The plan was they would complete all the forms on egg donation and then attend a counselling session.

Although the questions related to finding a matching donor were quite simple, i.e. what is the colour of your hair, Mr Moore? Alex had clearly gone into shutdown mode and was being particularly difficult.

"Mrs Moore, hair colour?"

"Blonde."

"Mr Moore?"

"Grey."

"Don't be stupid Alex, you weren't born with grey hair. It was black."

"I wasn't asked to give my hair colour at birth. In fact, I don't think I had any when I was born."

"Alex, can we just get on with this please."

"Mrs Moore, eye colour?"

"Blue, and his are brown."

"Bella, I do know the colour of my own eyes, thank you."

"It doesn't matter if the donor has blue or brown eyes in that case. I'll put both on the form."

"Whoa, yes it does."

Bella cringed, what on earth was Alex going on about now?

"I know it won't look like Bella but she's got blue eyes. I want a baby with my wife ideally, but if we can't I would at least like the donor to have blue eyes. I don't fancy brown-eyed girls as much. Mind you, though Emma Bunton gets my vote, Victoria Beckham is a bit of alright. I sort of had the blonde Swedish-look in the back of my mind."

The consultant laughed. At least he had a sense of humour. The problem was Alex wasn't joking. She had to have a serious word with him before they saw the counsellor.

The consultant completed the rest of the paperwork and they agreed to have Bella's hormones tested in two months' time.

Bella and Alex went back to the waiting room to wait for the counsellor.

As the room was empty, Bella decided to groom Alex so he performed well in front of the counsellor. She didn't want his flippant comments to affect their chances of being taken seriously.

"Alex, please behave in front of the counsellor. I don't want her to think we're unsuitable parents."

"Of course we're suitable parents Bella. I am just not sure about this whole egg donation thing, but if it's what you want...."

"Of course it's not what I want Alex. I want to get pregnant but as nobody seems able to confirm if we'll be able to use my eggs, this is the next best thing. I want to have your baby more that anything else in the world."

"Exactly, do you not think I want us to have a baby together more than anything else in the world? And if we have donated eggs, it wouldn't be part of you Bella, and I. don't think I can cope with that."

"Well as far as I'm concerned, it would be part of me. I'd be carrying the baby for nine months and giving birth to him or her. It would be my baby Alex, our baby."

"I don't actually think we'll need the donor eggs. The consultant said he could try different drugs and protocols. I reckon we'll make it Bella, seriously."

"I hope so Alex. I do feel a lot happier at this clinic."

Alex was on his best behaviour during the counselling session, and surprisingly the counsellor seemed pleased that they both agreed that they didn't believe in keeping secrets from children and would want to tell any future children conceived via egg donation of their special situation.

The counsellor seemed to understand that they'd prefer to have their own biological children and suggested that if that was not to be, then they would need time to accept their situation before entering into egg donation. She referred to it as having a grieving period. Bella hadn't thought of it that way.

They were accepted onto the list and the egg donation programme manager described various ways of recruiting donors. They were shown adverts in glossy magazines describing heartfelt pleas from couples desperate to recruit donors.

Bella imagined their advert penned by Alex.

"Childless couple desperately seeking a very attractive blue-eyed, blonde-haired Scandinavian au-pair preferably under 25 who would be willing to donate her eggs to help this worthy cause."

Bella made her mind up. This was Bella vs. Infertility - Round 2. She was going to do her best to make this next cycle work. This was it - no drinking, no kebabs, no stress, just yoga, crystals and meditation chants. Bring it on.

Chapter 17
Who's Sperm Is It Anyway?

Bella felt prepared for her second cycle of IVF. They both stopped drinking and Bella absorbed herself in alternative treatments. She even visited Tamsin's reflexologist. Bella felt great. They decided not to rush into the next cycle and wait until they both felt ready. Her hormone levels were steadily improving so they took time out with the consultant's blessing.

Bella was looking forward to the next cycle of IVF. She was convinced that the previous doctor didn't have a clue and this was a fresh start. The only slight problem was Alex. He seemed to be more stressed than ever with work. There had been two more cardboard box days and things weren't looking good. The costs were spiralling with Bella's quest to get pregnant. On Tamsin's advice, Bella was going to the reflexologist twice a week to calm her hormone levels down and that was not cheap.

Alex wasn't drinking in front of Bella, but on the odd night he was back late from work, Bella was sure she could smell stale alcohol on his breath. She decided to ignore it.

He was a lot better and it said in one of her books that stress was not good for her hormones so she just shut it out.

After two months of looking after herself, Bella felt a lot more prepared than last time. Bella was therefore not surprised to find out her blood test results were better, her hormones had improved. Maybe there was something in this alternative health after all. At least Alex couldn't knock it when he saw her credit card bills.

The clinic wanted to take a sample from Alex to check his sperm count was okay.

Bella had been trying his phone all afternoon and left several excited messages to confirm the improvement to her hormone results. She left several other messages telling him he needed to go and do one in the hospital cupboard and offered to courier an Argos catalogue to him.

Still no response. Bella was starting to get concerned.

Meanwhile, Alex was slumped in the corner of a bar in the City. He knew he was screwing up, but the bastards at work were getting to him. Bella was spending money on all sorts of crap and he needed to keep his job. It wasn't looking too hopeful. He received another earful from Dominic who made it clear his days were numbered. To make it worse, Bella left several messages on his phone. She sounded really excited, as her hormone results were much better. He felt awful. What if this was their last chance and he had screwed it up by drinking every day? He was too pissed to go to the clinic today. He could probably hide it at work but not at the hospital. Plus he doubted he could perform. Bella was going to kill him. What the hell was he going to do? He suddenly had an idea. It wasn't like they were going to use the sample today. They were only checking his count and potency. It wasn't like blood was it, surely they couldn't tell if it was his, plus he hadn't done a sample there before. He needed to make a phone call.

"Guy, it's me Alex."

"You sound a bit pissed my friend."

"I've just won a drinking competition with the boys."

"Well done old boy, what can I do for you?"

"A little favour my good pal. I need you to do a sperm sample at Redwoods for me."

"What? Are you out of your mind? What the hell will Jen say? Sorry I'm late darling, had to give Bella some sperm. No way, Alex. I have enough kids of my own. I can't believe you're asking me to do this."

"Don't be stupid. It's not what they'll use with the IVF cycle. It's just to see how my sperm count is. Bella's been working really hard to get her hormone levels right and they are the best ever and here I am pissed in a bar, too ashamed to even call her, let alone go for a sperm test. I'm telling you Guy, she would kill me if she knew. Please do this one thing for me, I'm begging you."

"You're a stupid bastard sometimes you know. I can't believe you're asking me to do this. Won't the hospital know it's not yours?"

"Look we'll go in together. The room is around the corner from reception. When they lead me round you pretend to go to the loo and nip into the room."

"Hang on a minute, you're going to be in the room with me? Are you warped? I really do think you've finally lost it."

"I'm not going to look, you idiot. I'm begging you Guy."

"What are the mags like?"

"Really good. I'll buy you some more on the way there, just in case."

"Okay deal, it could be quite a laugh. I tell you those nurses will fall off their perches when they see the quality of my sample."

"I owe you big time. Let's meet there at 3 p.m. I'll text Bella and say I'm too busy to call but I'll be going over later today to provide a sample. For God's sake, please promise not to tell Jen."

"Of course, don't forget the mags."

Bella was going to ask Alex to pick the drugs up from the hospital but as he wasn't answering his mobile and she needed to start sniffing that night, Bella decided to leave early and pick the drugs up herself.

Alex was feeling particularly nervous. He just wanted to get this over and done with and as usual, Guy was late.

Alex saw Guy jump off a bus opposite.

"Hi mate. Don't look so terrified Alex, it'll be fine. You look like you need some coffee."

Guy and Alex trudged up to the Assisted Conception Unit. Alex ate half a packet of extra strong mints in the lift.

Alex went to great pains to explain to the receptionist that Guy was visiting from overseas and he didn't want to leave him alone in London in case he got lost.

The receptionist didn't look too bothered.

It was all going to plan. Alex went into the room and shortly after Guy followed on the premise of finding the toilet.

"You made it, well done. I can't believe how many stares we were getting in the waiting room."

"Don't worry about it. Where's the pot and mags then?"

"Here you go."

Holding the receptacle to the light, Guy looked puzzled. "Blimey don't they have a bigger one?"

"No, Guy I can't believe it either. The jokers who designed this pot probably hailed from Lilliput. Last time round, I managed to get it stuck and I ended up nearly shattering the glass and imagined myself having to rush to A&E to have bits of broken glass removed from my appendage. At least I wouldn't have had too far to crawl. Now can you get on with it, and make sure it all lands in the pot! I'll face the other way and read 'The Sun'."

"Okay, Gulliver. I'll be quick, can't hang around here."

Alex was only halfway through the sports pages when Guy handed over the pot.

"Here you go mate. It'll be the best they've ever had."

"Look, you go now and I'll follow with the pot."

Bella raced up to the clinic to collect her drugs. It was so much better than last time. At least she had lost the 'no hope' badge she had been labelled with at the last clinic. She went past the reception to the pharmacy. Hang on a minute, what the hell was Guy doing here? He looked really hot and bothered.

"Guy what on earth are you doing here?"

Alex was staggering down the corridor holding onto his sperm pot. She could tell Alex was pissed. Something was wrong here – very wrong.

"Alex, what the hell's going on, you're drunk."

"Look I can explain, I er...got your message and was so pleased for you and your hormones, but I was having a really bad day and I know I shouldn't have had that extra beer at lunchtime. I just wanted my sperm to be okay, so I called Guy and asked him to come with me, you know, for morale support."

Bella looked at Guy who looked more than a little hot and flustered, surely not, even Alex would not stoop that low.

"Alex you're lying to me. Guy's done a bloody sample for you, hasn't he?"

"No way, of course not."

"Really Bella, what do you take me for? I know I'm a good mate of Alex's but I really would draw the line at that."

"Okay I'm sorry. I just cannot believe you've been drinking again Alex. I'm going to get the drugs, now wait outside because I want a serious chat with you."

Alex waited for Bella to go round the corner.

"Well done mate, she totally bought it. Wouldn't want to be in your house tonight though."

"I know, I'm going to get some serious grief. I just hope your test results are okay or I'll be even further in it."

"Jen's pregnant for the third time, of course they'll be okay. In fact, probably the best they've ever seen. Look, I'm going to leave you two to it. Tell Bella I had to go home as Jen has to go out."

"Okay mate, I owe you big time."

"Don't worry, I won't let you forget it."

Alex waited for Bella. How was he going to play this? It was no good pretending he hadn't been drinking, she had already clocked him. He was just going to have to go for the sympathy vote. That always worked with Bella. Alex figured he should leave the bit out about the drinking competition. Alex watched Bella come down the hospital steps. She didn't look too happy.

Alex decided to get in first.

"I know what you're going to say Bella, but when you hear about what happened today, believe me you'll understand."

"It better be good Alex, because I'm struggling to understand when I've been working really hard to get my hormones to the right level and have finally succeeded, why you're doing the one thing than could ruin our chances. So come on tell me, why did I find my husband staggering pissed around the corridors of the Assisted Conception Unit with his best mate?"

"Don't raise your voice in the street Bella, can we talk about it over a coffee?"

"I suggest we do, because if you were sober I would have suggested you went back to the clinic for training on the injections because these new drugs don't work with a gun. You've got to mix them every night and inject me in the stomach."

"Are you winding me up?"

"And with the state you seem to be in lately the very thought of it scares the life out of me. I think we need a chat, don't you?"

Alex hurried Bella into the nearest coffee bar and tried to carry the drinks without spilling them everywhere. His hands seemed to have taken on a life of their own.

"Look at you Alex, you're shaking like a leaf. That's what drink does to you, and you know what? I find it pathetic."

"Okay Bella let's just stop there. I know you've been working hard to sort your hormone levels out and the last thing in the world I would want is for me to screw things up for us now. I know I've been drinking too much again. It's just this whole work thing. Dominic told me today that he can't protect me any more and it looks like I'll be next out."

"You have no idea what it feels like Bella. They're scrutinising everything I do and I know they're just waiting to get me out. Every day I go into that place I know it could be my last and what makes it a hundred times worse is I know we need my job to fund the treatment. So there you go, I'm not coping right now, what else can I say?"

"But I need you to cope Alex, that's the problem. We can get through this and you know I'll support you but I don't want this situation with your job to cost us so dearly. This might be our only chance of having a child and I need you just to get through the next few weeks without drinking."

"I know you're right Bella, but I am finding this really tough. I've managed to hold down a job in the City for years.

I've seen loads of people come and go and I'm taking this really personally."

"Don't let them get to you, and for God's sake don't be so paranoid. Just focus on doing a good job and I'm sure they won't get rid of you. I booked an appointment with the nurse to have your training on the needles at 7:30 in the morning. I start sniffing at 7 p.m. tonight. Alex, I do love you and you know I'll support you but I need you now more than I've ever needed you. Please, for me, no drinking until we've finished this cycle."

"Bella, I won't let you down. I promise."

Bella heard this before but this time for the first time in her life she knew that if he ruined this, she would never forgive him. She hoped he would get it together not just for the sake of IVF but also for the sake of their marriage.

And God help him if Guy had produced the sample. She was still unconvinced.

Chapter 18
Stirrups and Probes

Bella stood outside the Assisted Conception Unit waiting for the moment of truth, the day seven scan. Had the drugs worked? Would she be like that smug fifteen-follicle bird, or would it be like before, one lonely follicle?

Alex stuck to his word and in fairness was being the model husband. Bella could tell that Alex was stressed but he was managing not to drink and was coping with mixing the injections every night. Alex did admit there was no way he could inject her stomach after ten pints of lager. While Bella saw this a bit of a breakthrough, she did stress that she felt he shouldn't even attempt it after one pint.

The only problem was Alex having to spend nearly every waking hour at work. His tactic was to throw everything at it on the basis that Bella could be right, they may not get rid of him just yet. Ideally he needed to hang in there until the treatment had been successful, then they would just have to manage until he found something else.

Bella felt so much better this time round. Whilst the drugs were still sending her a bit mental which she did acknowledge to herself while stroking numerous baby grows in Mothercare, she generally felt a lot calmer. It was only six weeks until Christmas. She kept imagining herself and Alex snuggled up on Christmas Eve patting her pregnant tummy.

In fact all was going well until Alex couldn't make the appointment for the scan. Unbelievably, Dominic had called a 7 a.m. breakfast meeting and the scan was at 8 a.m.

There was no way Bella could go on her own. What if she hadn't responded to the drugs again? After talking it through with Alex they agreed that Jen was probably the best person to go and Bella was waiting for her at the hospital. Jen managed to get the neighbour's au pair to look after Jake and Maddie so it was all sorted, at least Bella thought it was.

"Where's Jen?"

Bella was more than a little confused to see Guy running up the corridor.

"Why haven't you got your mobile on?" he asked.

"I'm in a hospital Guy, why do you think?"

"Jen's been calling you since 6 a.m. We had to have the emergency doctor out last night."

"Oh my God, is everyone okay?"

"Fine but the kids have chickenpox and Anya, next door's au-pair, hasn't had it so she can't look after them. Luckily both Jen and I have, but Jake has a high temperature and Jen is so sorry but she just can't leave him. She feels absolutely terrible doing this to you Bella."

"Please tell her not to worry, the main thing is that the kids are okay."

"I did offer to stay with them but you know what Jen's like, she thinks I'm useless with the kids, especially when they're ill."

"I'm sure she doesn't Guy. It's just sometimes they need their Mummy I guess."

"Look, enough of our problems, your scan's in five minutes. Do you want me to stay in the waiting room or would you prefer me to leave?"

"I need to explain to the receptionist as it looks a bit odd but would you mind staying?"

"Of course not."

Bella and Guy sat in the waiting room.

"Blimey Bella, you must be the youngest in here. Some of these are well past their sell-by date?"

"Keep your voice down Guy."

"Sorry, by the way was Alex's sperm test okay?"

"Yeah fine."

"Did they say anything about it? Was it better than last time?"

"Why are you so interested in Alex's sperm, Guy?"

"No reason. Just trying to be supportive that's all. "

The clinic was running late, typical. Bella was starting to get anxious. She had been so excited about her hormone levels she hadn't really contemplated failure. She still felt optimistic and hoped to God she wasn't heading for a big fall.

"What are they looking for on the scan?" asked Guy.

Bella wished Guy would shut up. She knew he meant well but she preferred just to read her book. She decided after the last clinic to distract herself by reading a book every time she had to wait so she could ignore everything going on around her. Guy was not making this easy.

"Grey blobs that are hopefully follicles that hopefully contain eggs that I can hopefully have removed to hopefully have fertilised to hopefully get pregnant."

"What if there aren't any then?"

"Well, I can't get pregnant then can I?"

"This is fairly major stuff today then?"

"That's one way of putting it Guy, yes."

"Do you want me to come in?"

126

"WHAT?"

"Don't shout, I'm used to scans. I know what's involved."

"Believe me this is nothing like a pregnancy scan. Does Jen have her feet in stirrups with a condom covered probe shoved up her whilst you watch an image of your unborn child?"

"Oh bloody hell, too much detail. I'll just stay in the waiting room if that's okay?"

"Fine by me, Guy."

She knew it wasn't Jen's fault but having Guy there was making things ten times worse plus everyone was now staring at them. Bella kept reminding herself to take her pop socks off. Last time she'd kept them on. If they were going to tell her she failed to respond to the drugs again at least she wanted to retain a little dignity. Pop socks in stirrups were not a good look.

They were now running fifteen minutes late.

"Does it hurt Bella?"

"Not physically Guy, no."

Guy kept trying to peer round the corner.

"I'm really nervous Guy, I want Alex."

Guy grabbed her hand.

"I don't think I can contact him Bella. Look you'll be fine. Both Jen and I have a good feeling about this."

"Really?"

"Honestly, you look so much better this time."

"I feel it. I just hope I don't go to pieces in there. I must remember to take my pop socks off."

"Are those the weird tight things like Jen wears that finish just below your knees?"

"That's them."

"Yes, I guess they could be pretty dangerous."

"What?"

The nurse interrupted Bella and Guy.

"Scan room number five please, Mrs Moore."

"Don't forget to take off your pop socks Bella. You don't want to slip out of the stirrups."

Bella could not believe Guy just shouted that across the waiting room. The morning was not going at all well.

Bella stripped from the waist down, she couldn't be bothered to listen to the nurse. She was focused on the screen. Was it her imagination or were there loads of grey blobs?

"You've responded well, Mrs Moore. There are eight follicles and they are all a good size. This is really good news.

Bella couldn't believe it.

"Does this mean we can do IVF?"

"Definitely. I'll just take some blood samples but everything is looking good. I reckon we'll be able to do egg collection in about five days time. I'd like you to come in for a scan every other day now until we schedule your egg collection."

Bella quickly got dressed and raced back to the waiting room, only to find Guy pacing up and down like he was waiting for Jen to give birth.

Bella was beaming.

"You've got eggs, haven't you?"

Bella laughed.

"Whoa."

After everything Bella had said to Alex when slagging off the fifteen-follicle bird and vowing that if she had success to keep it low key, she could not believe that Guy was swinging her around the waiting room. Alex should have been here.

Guy called Jen, whilst Bella texted Alex. They agreed he'd keep his phone on silent.

Eight follicles. Surely they would make it this time.

Chapter 19
The Next Miracle

The cycle was going well. Alex managed to administer the final injection before egg collection without stabbing either himself or Ginger.

Alex seemed calmer about work. He was putting in longer hours than usual and seemed convinced he could hang in for a few more months. Following Tamsin's advice, Bella had booked three days holiday - one for egg retrieval and two to rest afterwards. Alex had taken a day's holiday. They had to be at the hospital by 7 a.m.

Bella was feeling a bit nervous. She wasn't worried about having the general anaesthetic, she was just hoping there were actually eggs in there. After all this she didn't think she could cope if there weren't. The consultant has assured her that she would be the first one down to theatre and he would stop by once she came round to let her know how things had gone.

Bella was ready in her theatre gown. Alex thought it was highly amusing that it didn't fasten too well and her ever-expanding bottom was hanging out the back.

"I can't believe you're eating a sausage sandwich Alex. It's making me feel sick. It's hardly a good time."

"I always eat when I'm stressed."

"Try not to worry about it Alex, I'm not at all concerned about the medical procedure. I just hope they find some eggs."

"I'm not worried about that."

"What exactly is bothering you, Alex?"

"Well it's alright for you, at least you don't have to do anything other than lie there. You're hardly under pressure to perform. What if I can't?"

"Oh Alex, please don't say that, you're starting to make me feel sick. Of course you'll perform."

"Yeah right, no pressure."

"Guy's given me some better magazines. He had to get rid of some because Maddie brought 'Hot Housewives' downstairs to show the health visitor when they were doing Jake's eight-month development review. Jen went mad apparently. He promised to get rid of them and so he saved them for our special moment. You're right, I'll be fine."

"Mrs Moore, time to take you down to theatre."

Alex mouthed good luck, at least she thought he did, but his mouth was full of sausage. He also waved a copy of 'Hot Housewives' and winked. Bella could not believe this. She was actually starting to look forward to the anaesthetic.

The team in the theatre was jolly, like over-hyped Easter Bunnies about to start an Easter egg hunt. They wished Bella good luck. They needed it more than she did, thought Bella. They obviously didn't realise today's egg hunt could be more than a challenge. They started to count down from ten. Bella drifted off at eight.

⤸

Bella started to stir. The whole thing must have been really quick. The Easter Bunnies were running around wrapping her in tin foil stuff. Apparently her temperature had dropped. Bella really didn't care about her temperature. When were they going to tell her about the eggs?

They returned her back to the room where Alex was pacing with a family size bag of crisps in his hand.

"Bella darling, are you okay? Why are you wrapped in tin foil?"

"Don't know. My temperature dropped apparently. Did 'Hot Housewives' work? Have you seen the consultant yet?"

"Yes, it went well. I nearly filled the pot. Anyway the consultant will be round in thirty minutes. Do you want a crisp?"

"No thanks, I feel a bit groggy."

"You have a sleep. I'll wake you up when the consultants arrive."

Bella fell in and out of a deep sleep. She was aware of Alex crunching crisps and various hospital staff coming and going but she was in a comfortable state of semi-consciousness.

"Bella, Bella, guess what he's been in. They got eight. Can you believe it! Eight! This could be it Bella. Apparently my sperm are performing like Olympian athletes. I have such a good feeling about this. We can go any time now and they'll call to let us know how many have fertilised. Apparently they'll call between 9 a.m. and midday to let us know. You have to make sure you're there to take the call. This is so exciting, Bella!"

Bella couldn't believe it. She just needed them to fertilise. IVF was unbelievable. You're always waiting for the next miracle.

Chapter 20
Brown Box Day

The next miracle arrived. Alex took the call whilst Bella hid her head under the pillows. Six eggs had fertilised. They decided to transfer two and freeze the remaining four, just in case. Bella arranged to meet Alex at the hospital for the embryo transfer. The best two were chosen - one was six cells and one was four. Bella remembered the consultant saying the embryo transfer would be painless, just legs in stirrups while a catheter is inserted to pop them in.

Bella couldn't believe it - pop them in, pop what in, their two babies? So far this IVF cycle had been fine, not that painful and they'd actually got as far as embryo transfer. This was the closest they'd ever been. Bella could hardly contain her excitement. Jen was sorting out some old baby stuff on the basis that she and Guy just found out they were having a girl, so Jake's clobber was redundant.

Bella was due to meet Alex at 1 o'clock for the transfer. Bella told Anthony she had a hospital appointment and needed half a day off. Tamsin advised her against going straight back to work after the transfer and loaned her some whale music and blue candles so she could spend the afternoon meditating. Bella wasn't sure how to mediate but she'd bought a copy of OK and a Kit Kat and assumed it would be the next best thing.

Bella was sat in the waiting room. It was 1:05 p.m. and still no Alex. Bella tried to discreetly call him from her mobile. Surely he wasn't going to miss this. This was the closest they'd ever been to the conception of their child. The receptionist informed Bella they could only give it until 1:15 p.m. due to the number of embryo transfers taking place. Where the hell was Alex? It was now 1:14 p.m. and he was nowhere to be seen. My God, she was going to have to go it alone? Bella started to panic. She hoped he was okay. Alex had been so excited about the transfer. He'd read on the leaflet from the hospital that you actually got to see the embryos on a screen before they went in.

Bella reluctantly went into the room for the transfer. They were crosschecking all the information when a stressed out Alex shot into the room. Bella instantly smelt stale beer and fags - bastard.

"I am so sorry. Can't believe I nearly missed this. Have they been on the screen yet?"

"Where have you been? You just made it on time, Alex. Sit down, you're making me feel sick swaying around so much."

"Sorry."

The embryologist was busily cross-referencing the details.

"Alex, why are you drunk?"

"I'm not, I only had one for luck."

"Listen, I'm not prepared to argue at what could be our nearest attempt at a romantic conception in Bali, i.e. me in stirrups, you pissed and two grey blobs on a screen that could be our future children."

"I agree, let's make it romantic."

"Make the most of it Alex, because when I get you out of here romance will be the last thing on the agenda."

Alex held Bella's hand while they completed the transfer. It was quite nice and Bella felt all floaty like she had butterflies in her stomach, maybe this was it.

Bella thanked the consultant and they left the room.

"Hang on, Bella, I've left something behind in reception."

Bella would have to forgive him. She had a sneaky suspicion he left some flowers for her behind the reception, which was typical of Alex. How could she berate him now for being drunk at the embryo transfer? Alex appeared round the corner with a huge brown box. Bella instantly knew what that meant. That bastard Dominic, not today.

"Sorry Bella, that's why I've had a drink. Bastard fired me this morning. Said he'd tried to do everything to save me but my time had run out, no more excuses. I'm so sorry."

Bella felt the butterflies disappear. She felt empty. She realised they were standing outside in the pouring rain.

Alex was trying to get a cab.

"We can't afford a cab if you're not working Alex. We'll have to get the bus."

"Don't be foolish. The money hasn't run out yet, plus I want you to rest with that elephant music Tamsin gave you."

"It's whale music, Alex."

They jumped into a cab.

"You think it's my fault, don't you?" he asked.

"Today is the happiest day I've had in years and that bloody git Dominic has ruined it."

"I've got a really good feeling about this, Bella. Hopefully you won't need any more treatment and I'll get another job. Don't panic."

"Can't Andrew get you something at his bank?"

"There's no way I'm begging Andrew. Honestly Bella, things aren't that bad yet."

"What if we have twins, I won't be able to work."

"We'll find a way. I just want to focus on looking after you and the embryos. What should we call them? Embie One and Embie Two?"

"Whatever, Alex, I just can't think straight. I'm going to get at one with Tamsin's whale music and try and relax. Embie One and Two should be our priority now."

"Exactly, so please stop stressing about my job. In a way I'm more relaxed now, as I've had the hatchet hanging over my neck for months. You don't realise the effect this has had on me."

"On us, Alex, it has had an effect on both of us. The best thing you can do now is just leave me alone to rest. I need some quiet time with the embies."

Chapter 21
Two Weeks Wait

Bella could not believe how slowly the days were passing. They had a two-week wait before they would know if the treatment had been successful. Alex was being impossible. He was in the City every day drinking and Bella was finding it difficult to even be civil. Headphones and whale music were forming a key part of shutting out Alex and the crap that was going on in their marriage.

Bella watched Tamsin flounce into Trepido. She had received an email from Tamsin earlier titled The Two Week Wait with a request for a lunch appointment.

"Darling how are you doing?"

"Not good, I cannot believe how this is dragging on, Tamsin. It feels like the longest two weeks of my life."

"I know, just try and stay positive."

"I'm trying. I'm doing the whale CD and candle thing every night and I'm trying not to let work stress me out."

"Great, you're doing all the right things."

"Yes, but I'm really worried. I don't feel any different. I've stopped the mind-bending drugs. I just feel normal. Shouldn't I be throwing up or weeing every 5 minutes?"

"Don't worry about looking for signs of being pregnant, it's way too early plus everyone has different pregnancy symptoms."

"I don't feel any different than when I had the turkey basting. I hoped having little embies inside me that at least I'd experience that whole 'I've got something living inside me' feel. With IVF it's like you think you might be pregnant before you ever know if you conceived normally."

"Am I making sense?"

"I know, I've been there."

"Honestly Tamsin girl to girl, what happens if you lose them, is it a miscarriage?"

"Difficult, that one. I never got a positive pregnancy test. So I must have lost them before they implanted. Technically, I guess it's not a miscarriage but knowing you have lost them makes you feel like you've had one. It's really difficult and I think it's only something you can relate to if you've experienced IVF. I remember telling people that my IVF failed and the general response was 'oh well, better luck next time', yet if I told people I'd had a miscarriage – total sympathy because people can relate to that. It's the loss of a life whereas to us, losing embryos is a loss of life but people just can't relate to that."

"I guess you're right. I can't believe I'm asking you this, but how do you know if they've died?"

"You don't, well certainly I didn't until I got my period. Normally the period from hell by the way. But honestly Bella, don't you think you are jumping ahead?"

"Sorry, I just can't believe I feel nothing, like I'm empty inside. Do you think I could have lost them?"

"Relax, you won't know for another 10 days so don't add any more stress to the situation."

"You're right. It's stressful at home with Alex and I think it's all starting to get on top of me. It was going so well and now look at us. Alex lost his job and I'm obsessing about losing these embies."

"Oh Bella, I'm sorry I didn't realise Alex lost his job."

"Yeah, it's been on the cards a while. The trouble is he says he's going into the City every day looking for work, but he just comes home smelling of drink. If I lose the embies, he'll go into meltdown. He seems to have lost all of his self-esteem since they fired him. He avoids telephone calls, he hasn't even told his batty old mother yet. What makes it worse is I don't feel I can support him. I want to slap him and tell him to get a job and sort his life out. I don't feel I can take any more on. I want to focus on getting pregnant and let him deal with the rest. I know I should be more supportive but I can't find it within myself at the moment. Do you think I'm a total bitch?"

"Of course I don't think that. IVF puts the best relationships under incredible pressure. It's like being on a roller coaster. The problem is, Bella, I only allowed room in my life for IVF, work and nothing else. I think that's why Rod left me in the end. We ended up having relationship counselling and it became clear that Rod no longer felt he had a place in my life. So he shagged a much younger version of me."

"What worries me Tamsin is if this fails I've got to go through another gruelling cycle of this. They've already said we can't leave too much of a gap due to the question over my eggs and I don't think I can do it. I don't think I can go through another month of worrying whether Alex is going to even turn up at clinic appointments, let alone administer injections after ten pints. I do love him but I can't see it working unless I get pregnant this time."

"You're putting yourself under a lot of pressure. What are you saying, if this fails no more IVF or no more Alex?"

"No, to both."

"Whoa Bella, it's not a good time to be making these sort of decisions. Why don't you wait to see what happens with the IVF and then consider your next step. This is really one day at a time stuff. Don't do anything too rash."

"I won't. I do love him Tamsin, but I'm not sure I can take much more. But you're right, I should wait. I cannot believe I've told you all of this. I haven't told anyone else. I don't feel anyone else can relate to what I'm going through. Sorry to burden you though."

Bella was sobbing uncontrollably. When were her hormones going to calm down?

"You're not a burden. I want you to know you can call me if you ever need to talk. Just think about what you're doing. You don't want to have any regrets."

"Ladies, good to see you two bonding."

Oh my God, thought Bella. What the hell was Anthony doing in here?

"Bella, what on earth are you doing sobbing? Tamsin is a client. We must remember to be professional at all times."

Just as Bella was about to apologise, Tamsin took control in her own inimitable style.

"Sod off Anthony, we're busy. Oh and don't have a go at Bella afterwards. This is between her and me, and has nothing to do with work. In fact, Bella is the one reason we keep our business with your lousy company. She's the only one who actually gets the job done. So don't even think about upsetting her – got it?"

Anthony shuffled off towards the bar. This was, albeit in bizarre circumstances, the only positive thing Tamsin had ever said about her. Her life was getting stranger by the minute. Bella thanked Tamsin again and went back to her desk. She spent the rest of the afternoon deflecting missiles from one of the new assistants who didn't know an aircraft from a train, and avoiding Anthony.

Bella dreaded going home. She knew Alex had been "networking" in the City again. The only problem was his network only seemed to consist of pub landlords. She couldn't believe the words came out of her mouth today. She was contemplating leaving Alex and she told Tamsin. Who else was she going to talk to? All her friends were friendly with both of them and other than Guy, Jen, Andrew and Susannah none of them knew about the IVF. It was no good telling her parents. Her mother would have it on the agenda at the golf club AGM. Forget it, she would have to go this alone. If she was going to leave him she could suggest they have a break and then see if he sorts himself out. It could go one of two ways, but if he didn't get himself sorted, how the hell would they get through IVF again, especially with all of the drinking? He had been drinking solidly since the transfer of embie one and two and Bella had to endure the whisky breath as he talked to her tummy every night.

If embie one and two made it, he would have to sort himself out. There was no way Bella was bringing any child or children into this mess. The drinking would have to stop and he would have to get a job. Either way, Bella felt they needed some space.

Chapter 22
All Bets Are Off

It was e-day as Alex put it. Had embie one and two made it? The two weeks were up and guess what, no period. Bella was trying not to get too excited.

It was Saturday afternoon and Alex was still in his pyjamas in front of the television. He must have asked her sixty times how she was feeling.

"How are you feeling?"

Make that sixty-one.

"Same as last time. I've just had another good luck text from Jen."

"Shall I go out and get a pregnancy test, or do you have a stock of them still? Do you think we should do a test today?"

"I thought we'd leave the test for now. I think you can get a false positive after IVF so I'd rather wait until the blood test on Monday."

"Oh okay, do you think I should put some champagne in the fridge?"

"As I might not be pregnant and on the basis that you don't have a job, I don't think that would be such a good idea, do you?"

"For God's sake, Bella, will you stop snapping at me. Nothing I do lately is right."

"That's maybe why I snap at you, Alex."

"What are you trying to say Bella, just come right out with it will you."

"Okay this is what I'm trying to say Alex, I'm sympathetic about your job."

"Liar."

"Will you please allow me to finish. I feel you're totally out of control. Alex, you spend your days hiding behind a pint glass and don't tell me that you've been trying to get a job. It's a load of crap. You haven't been for an interview and you expect me to go to work and try to get through this whole IVF thing whilst you prop up a bloody bar every day. So that's how it is Alex, got it?"

"You're not supporting me Bella."

"This is about doing it for yourself, for me and for embie one and two. I thought you'd pull yourself together. I've always supported you Alex but this time you need to do it for yourself."

"So I'm on my own now, is that what you're saying? Do you want me to leave, would that make it easier Bella?"

Bella was about to reply when she felt a searing pain in her stomach. Oh God no.

"Do you want me to go Bella? At least answer the bloody question."

Bella bolted upstairs to the bathroom. She pulled her jeans and knickers down.

"Don't hide in there Bella, just give me a straight answer will you?"

Bella looked up at the sky before she looked down. "Please help me God, please don't let them go."

"Bella what is it?"

Bella looked down. The mess confirmed her worst fears, embie one and two hadn't made it. She could barely breathe. She unlocked the bathroom door and Alex rushed in. He saw her face and looked down. Alex grabbed her and they both fell to their knees sobbing.

Bella eventually picked herself up off the floor.

"I'm going to bed Alex."

"Bella, I'm so sorry this is all my fault. If only I'd have kept my job and not been drinking. Do you think we lost them because of all the stress? I shouldn't have shouted at you Bella. I'm so sorry. I'll never forgive myself for this."

"Just give me some space, Alex."

"You do blame me, don't you? I can see it in your eyes. I never meant for this to happen. I wanted embie one and two more than anything in the world. I want to make you happy Bella; you know how much I love you. Please forgive me."

"I don't want to talk about this now Alex. I just want to lie down, please leave it."

Bella threw the whale CD across the bedroom, the stupid thing. She heard the front door slam. Probably Alex going off to the pub. She didn't blame Alex. They always knew the odds were low. Bella thought of Alex's roulette comparison. It was never going to be an easy win. However, it didn't stop her wondering if things could have been different. What if he'd towed the line? Was stress a contributor with this whole IVF thing? The truth is they would never know. But either way right now she knew she couldn't do another cycle of IVF. No way. No bloody way.

Bella could hear someone banging at the door. Surely Alex wasn't too drunk to get the key in the lock. She hauled herself out of bed and opened the front door. Bella had spent what seemed like hours holding her knees to her chest and rocking, she was too exhausted to cry. Bella was not prepared to meet Alex, Guy, Jen and the kids.

Jen took control.

"Can we come in?"

Bella panicked. "It's not my turn to host supper is it?"

"No, it's just that Alex was really worried and you're not answering the phone."

Bella let them in. She just didn't need this, not tonight. Typical bloody Alex.

"Aunty Bella, why are you in your pyjamas, it's not bedtime yet?"

Jen quickly grabbed the children.

"Be quiet Maddie, go and play on the rug with Jake. Sorry Bella we couldn't leave them anywhere at such short notice. I thought we could leave the kids in here while we all have a chat in the kitchen. "

Alex and Guy hadn't spoken yet. Jen seemed to be taking control and made them all a cup of tea while they sat around the kitchen table in silence.

Bella wasn't sure which way this was going to go. She wondered if Alex had already been out and about building a coalition whilst she was sleeping in her 'Winnie The Pooh' pyjamas. No doubt he'd already laid it on thick. "It's failed and Bella blames me," she could just hear it. Bella did feel extremely vulnerable and the pyjamas weren't helping.

Bella knew Jen would take the lead.

"Listen, we know Bella, Alex told us that the IVF cycle failed and we're very sorry. Try and stay positive Bella, look how you bounced back last time."

Bella couldn't believe it.

"I don't think you understand. This isn't like last time. Last time was admittedly a spectacular failure, but this time we've seen our embryos on the screen. Embryos Alex and me had made. Our embryos and I have lost them. You've no idea how that feels, so please don't sit there whilst your two kids play in the lounge and tell me to bounce back. What would you say if I'd had a miscarriage? I wouldn't be told to bounce back then, would I?"

Alex started to look uneasy.

"Bella please don't shout at Jen. We're all trying our best. Jen and Guy have something they want to ask us."

"Sorry, but it's not a good day to ask if we'll be Godparents again."

"Bella please, go on Jen."

"Listen Bella, Guy and I have been talking about your situation and we're desperately sorry things haven't worked out this time and I'm sorry if I have said the wrong thing today. Anyway, we've been talking and I didn't want to say anything until we knew about the outcome of this treatment but if it comes to it and you can't have any more IVF, I would be more than happy to donate some of my eggs. We've talked it through and we're not sure how it would all work, but basically Guy and I are willing to do this if you'd like us to help."

Bella was speechless. It was the nicest thing anybody ever offered to do for her but the thought of Alex and Jen sort of having a baby together, she just could not get her head around it and unknown to any of them she couldn't go through IVF again, not with Alex in the state he was in.

"Well, say something Bella," snapped Alex

What did Alex expect her to say? What did Guy and Jen expect her to say? They just offered them Jen's eggs, not a glass of wine."

"I'm sorry guys. I'm just completely overwhelmed by your act of kindness. Well it's more than that. I'm sorry I had a go at you earlier Jen. It's really tough at the moment. I guess we all need time to think this through. I don't want to appear to be ungrateful because believe me, I'm not. It's the most wonderful thing anyone has ever offered. I'm just not sure I can go through IVF again."

Alex looked surprised.

"You didn't tell me you were feeling like this Bella."

"You have been out all afternoon Alex. I've hardly had a chance."

"What about the ones we've got on ice? We've got another two shots at this and if that fails, we know we can rely on Jen."

Guy suddenly became very animated.

"You've got frozen babies?"

Jen glared at Guy.

"Shut up Guy for God's sake"

"We had four embryos frozen," Bella couldn't believe they were getting into all this.

"Wow, how does that work then? Are they in the freezer?"

Jen was looking increasingly annoyed.

"They defrost them and put them into Bella to see if they survive. They're in the freezer at the lab not amongst our frozen oven chips and pizza."

"Wow"

Bella felt like they were in a science class and she was the live experiment.

"It's not that easy, they don't always survive the thawing process and I think the odds on a frozen cycle are far less than on a fresh."

Alex put his head in his hands. "It has to be worth a go Bella, we can't just leave them there."

"Alex will you please drop it. I'm not ready to make those decisions yet. I've only just lost the other two okay. I'm not sure if I can take any more pain or any more failure, especially considering how things are at the moment."

"Another cheap shot at me, great. Don't you think I'm devastated over this as well?"

"Oh stop feeling so bloody sorry for yourself Alex."

"And don't you go banging on about a miscarriage to Jen when she's only trying to help."

"Right, that's it."

Bella stormed out of the kitchen, she wasn't staying around to hear this. She raced upstairs, that was it, the final straw. She wanted out of here. She needed some space away from Alex, away from all the desperation and drama. Bella started to grab things out of her wardrobe and throw them into a bag. She needed time out.

A tearful Jen appeared at the door.

"What the hell's going on Bella?"

"I'm leaving, that's what's going on."

"Isn't this a bit sudden? You and Alex have always been so strong. You can get through anything you two."

"Maybe, but right now I need time away from all this."

"Where are you going to go?"

"No idea, not sure if they do a hostel for infertile women?"

"I don't think this is a good time to go Bella. Your hormones must be in a right state. I just think you're being too hasty. At least talk to Alex, he's in pieces down there. He knows you're going to leave him. He thinks he's going to lose you for good. You know how much he loves you."

Bella collapsed on the bed sobbing.

"I know Jen, I just want time away from all of this to think, and maybe it will be good for him too. Maybe the only way for him to sort his life out is to give him some space to think."

"Do you blame him for the treatment failing?"

"No, not really. I blame him for not sorting his life out. He has been drinking right the way through this cycle. He's hardly been supportive."

"But look at what's happened with his job. It's really hard on men, that type of stuff, it dents their ego."

"Oh here we go again, let's all feel sorry for Alex. Look Jen, I am sorry he's lost his job but he needs to sort himself out and if I stay here I'll just be his emotional crutch again and I need some time for myself. He needs to do this for himself. I'm going to leave, that doesn't mean I'm not going to come back, but I want to give him the chance and the space to sort himself out."

Alex appeared round the bedroom door, he looked terrible.

"Please don't go, I'm begging you Bella, I'll do anything."

"I think a break would be good for both of us Alex."

Jen quickly left the bedroom.

"You still love me don't you Bella? I still love you."

"Of course I do, but if you truly love me please give me the space I need and try to sort yourself out Alex."

"You will come back won't you?"

The tears were streaming down Alex's cheeks.

"If you sort yourself out Alex, yes."

"I will Bella, I promise. Where are you going to go? You're still in your pyjamas."

"Can you get Jen?"

"Sure."

"Come on Bella get dressed, you're coming home with me and Guy. You can stay with us until you get sorted."

"That's going to make it really difficult for Guy and Alex, don't worry I'll find somewhere."

"I won't take no for an answer. I can't have you trying to find somewhere to live in this state and neither can Alex. You're coming to stay with us and that's final. I'll get Guy to load your bags whilst I tell the kids."

Bella hugged Ginger. As she was making the first move she didn't feel she could ask Alex to leave. It was down to her. They loaded up the car. The kids seemed excited by the prospect of Aunty Bella coming to stay.

Alex came to the front door.

"I don't want to have a big goodbye session on the doorstep Alex, it's only temporary until you get yourself sorted. Can we just leave it at that?"

They were both crying.

"Please don't go Bella, I'm begging you. We can sort this out."

"Don't Alex."

"I love you Bella."

"I love you too."

Bella squeezed in the back seat with a very excited Jack and Maddie. She couldn't bear to look at Alex as they pulled away. It was just too raw.

Chapter 23
Three Parts Gin, One Part Tonic

"Aunty Bella, me show you my dancing, now. Now Aunty Bella."

Bella looked at her watch - it was 6 a.m. Normally it would be Ginger nibbling her feet looking for food. Now it was Maddie in her tutu about to start a command performance. Bella felt sick. She had left Alex. In the cold light of day it was incredibly scary.

Jen bustled in.

"Maddie, go and show Daddy your dancing please. Aunty Bella is very tired."

Maddie exited with a clumsy pirouette taking with her most of Bella's make up.

"How are you doing Bella?"

"Crap, I can't believe it Jen. I've left him."

"I know. If you're having second thoughts Bella, just call him. Maybe being away for one night was enough to show him you're serious, it kind of sends a message, like a warning shot. Why don't you just go home?"

"No, I know Alex too well. He'll be the adoring husband for a week and if things don't go his way on the job front, he'll be propping up the bar again."

"You need to think this through Bella. If you don't want this to be permanent don't you think you should be at home supporting him? What are we saying here, has he got a drink problem? Do you think he needs help?"

"I'm too weak to support anyone at the moment. I'm sorry if that sounds selfish but I need to come to terms with the fact this has failed before I take on Alex's problems. No, I just want to see how things go, take a breather for a month and then take it from there."

"Your call. How would you feel if he met someone else?"

"What, Alex? He's normally too pissed."

"Don't assume he won't. Someone might think he's a good catch."

"I'd be angry. We're supposed to be working things out not going out on a shag fest."

"Right, so you clearly don't want it to end then. Just watch yourself Bella. You are both really vulnerable right now and, well, you know how weak men can be."

"I don't intend to spell it out to him. I'm still going to call him every day and if he sorts himself out he can take me on a date if he wants, you know build up gradually. I also need to find somewhere to live."

"Don't worry about that, you can stay here as long as you want."

"I can't Jen, it's not fair on you and Guy. I'd rather set a time and then we all know what we're getting into and of course I'll pay you rent."

"I tell you what, let's say a month and sod the rent, you can do the babysitting, deal?"

"Deal."

"I don't suppose you fancy coming Christmas shopping?"

"No. It's going to make me miss Alex more. I was hoping we would be spending this Christmas stroking my baby bump, not living apart. I tell you what, you and Guy go shopping and I'll have the kids."

"That would be fantastic. We could get so much more done. I'll write you a list of instructions. It might be quite a challenging day."

"No more challenging than living with Alex, believe me."

Bella had a day of complete chaos. Jen and Guy had totally taken advantage of the free time and Bella calculated she had spent eight hours with Jake and Maddie. She was incredibly fraught. It was 5 o'clock and she realised she hadn't even spoken to Alex. Jake and Maddie were throwing food at each other in the kitchen and Bella decided it was time to call while they were occupied.

"It's me, just called to see how you were doing?"

"I'm doing fine really considering our IVF failed yesterday, my wife left me, I have no job and could be according to you an alcoholic."

"Don't be so dramatic, Alex."

Jake started screaming.

"Oh Maddie, no darling you mustn't throw your bowl at Jake's head, please try and only throw the food it doesn't hurt him so much."

"Have Guy and Jen left you with the kids?"

"Yes, I'm babysitting in lieu of rent until we're sorted."

"Does that mean you are coming back then?"

"If you sort your act out Alex, so I know I can come back and not have all the stress again, then I'll be back."

"So, what have I got to do? Get a job, stop drinking, get a life and improve my sperm, anything else?"

"Sounds like you've got it."

"Is there a timeframe? I mean it's two weeks before Christmas. Or am I spending Christmas alone with Ginger?"

"Alex, don't panic about Christmas just focus on fixing these problems."

"What about your problems Bella? You've given me a list, and I'd like to do the same."

"Okay Alex, go for it."

"Firstly, you have to stop obsessing about being pregnant. I would rather live with my wife than a living and breathing egg timer. Secondly, you need to support me more. The whole time I've been going through hell at work and you have no idea what it's been like because you never asked me. So long as we could get through a cycle of IVF, then that was all that mattered. Thirdly, I hate it when you paint your nails in bed. The fumes are disgusting from that stuff. Okay?"

"How the hell did you expect me to help you Alex when you weren't even helping yourself? I'm not saying what happened at work was your fault but my God, drinking to blot it out hardly helped and please don't say it was me and my nail varnish that tipped you over the edge. How did you expect me to cope with working full-time and going through the physical and emotional roller-coaster of IVF and propping you up?"

"What I'm saying Bella is there's not been room for anything in your life other than IVF. You spend hours on the internet, you drag Jen to support groups, you even have infertility coffee mornings with one of your clients and where do I fit in? Other than in the bloody sperm cupboard at the hospital, nowhere."

"I know this has taken over my life but do you think that's what I want? I've tried to fight this and I'm exhausted. I'm completely burnt out. There's always been room for you except when you drink and ruin everything we're working so hard to achieve – a baby. Until we have tried everything, I don't feel I can accept a life without children and I feel you're stopping us trying another cycle of IVF because I can't possibly contemplate it with you in the state you're in."

"Are you going to come home?"

"I think we need time apart, it's for the best Alex."

"How much time? What about my Christmas lunch?"

Bella could not believe he was already panicking about who was going to cook the turkey.

"I'm not sure, we'll see how it goes. I'll call my parents tonight and let them know I'm staying at Jen and Guy's for a while. Don't worry, I'm not going to go into any detail."

"Okay I love you and Ginger misses you terribly."

"Don't use Ginger Alex."

"In what way, are you saying I should register him with the CSA, Cats Support Agency? That's a point as I am not earning and you have left me you should be really paying maintenance for him, he was your baby replacement not mine. I hate the four- pawed little monster. Would Jake and Maddie like him as a Christmas present? It's all I can afford on the Jobseekers Allowance "

"Look I've got to go, Jake and Maddie are about to kill each other."

"Okay, will you call me every day?"

"Of course."

Bella heard the front door slam.

"Hello Guy, good shop?"

"Bella darling, sorry we have been so long. Did the Christmas shopping, went for a quick one, had a row over the kids and got a bit pis…Maddie let go of Jake's throat. Bet you had a crap day, sorry."

"Compared to a day fuelled by IVF drugs, clients fuelled by drugs and a husband fuelled by alcohol, this was bliss."

"Still not back with Alex then?"

"No, but don't worry I won't be staying long."

"I didn't mean that it just means, well, it's going to screw Alex up even further. He does love you Bells, you know that."

"He just needs to prove it Guy. He knows how much I want to keep trying for a baby and he knows I cannot do it in the state he's in and let's face it, we all know I haven't got time on my side."

"No pressure then."

"I know it's going to be tough for him, it's tough for both of us, Guy."

Jen rushed in and hugged Maddie and Jake. They were still plastered in food from the earlier food fight.

"Bella, I'm so sorry. I'm going to bath these two. Guy will get you a gin and tonic."

"Yes, boss."

"Would you prefer to bath the kids Guy?"

"No, I'd rather be bartender, thanks."

Guy waited for Jen to leave with Jake and Maddie.

"Well, don't think when the kids arrive it answers everything. You know 2.2 kids and an estate car doesn't always mean marital bliss."

"You and Jen seem to be fine, in chaos but fine."

"Things aren't always what they seem Bella."

"Oh come on, you two are great together. Look at the problems Alex and I have. It kind of puts your marriage in perspective."

"She just takes over with the kids. It's like I'm bloody inept, at least she thinks I am. Plus they are her life now, have you noticed? She's been in bloody jogging bottoms for the last 3 years and if she gets a spare minute, she's reading Mother & Baby."

"Guy, please don't do this. If you've got issues with Jen, please talk to her not me. She has been so good to me with the IVF thing. I'm sure if you let her know how you feel, she'll take it on board. You are having your third child and all three have been virtually back-to-back. No wonder she's still in jogging bottoms. I doubt I would have even been out of my dressing gown."

"That's the problem, she's always been so capable that she makes everyone around her feel useless. When I feed the kids I haven't the right spoon or I get the angle of Jake's beaker wrong. Anyway, enough of my crap. Fancy a G&T old girl?"

"Please, large."

"Don't worry, I know the strength when you've had the kids all day - 3 parts gin, 1 part tonic."

"Shall I start some food while Jen does the kids?"

"Don't worry, put your feet up. Captain Capable will be down in a second to cook a gourmet feast whilst she sterilises the bottles and makes a fancy dress outfit for Maddie. Come on, we'll go in the sitting room and watch TV."

Bella sat on the sofa with her XL G&T. She couldn't believe she had walked out of one domestic drama into another.

Chapter 24
Tambourines and Trailer Parks

Bella opened an email from Tamsin entitled 'NEED YOU IN MIAMI OR ANTHONY DIES'. She decided to grab a coffee before investigating further. Previously before considering any travel crises, Bella would be checking her red stars in her diary to see if she could make the trip without conflicting with her fertile peaks. Fertile peaks, what a joke! At least now she didn't have to worry about that.

It had been an interesting week. Bella managed to field regular calls from her mother who was concerned that she might meet someone of slightly less social standing than Alex. Bella assured her she didn't feel she could go much lower than an unemployed alcoholic but she'd let her know if the opportunity arose.

Even Alex's mad mother called her and begged her to take him back because "he wasn't eating properly." Everyone seemed to feel sorry for Alex. He managed to agree with Guy and Jen that he would come over for Christmas Day on the premise that he wouldn't drink and would be civil to Bella. Even Ginger secured a bloody invite, as Alex felt guilty leaving him home on his own. They had bonded since Bella's departure.

Bella was feeling increasingly uncomfortable at Guy and Jen's. It had been 9 days and 4 hours since she left Alex and 7 days to go until Christmas. She had to move after Christmas. It was bizarre but Guy seemed to spend most evenings in the lounge sipping a G&T with Bella while Jen ran round like a lunatic. Despite Bella pleading with Jen to allow her to help, Jen seemed determined to steam on regardless. Guy relished any opportunity to moan about how neglected he felt and how Jen had created a world around the children and pushed him out. Bella had enough problems of her own without listening to Guy every night. Even the thought of staying with her parents was becoming more appealing.

Bella decided to open the Miami email.

Darling,

You know we have the music awards in Miami in January? Well my boss has decided he wants someone there from the travel side to help with the artists. Last year was just a nightmare, too many tantrums not enough hands. Anyway he has invited Anthony.

Well, I have thrown one of my fits. There is no way I'm having Anthony on site. He will panic at the slightest thing and I'm very concerned that I won't be able to restrain myself if he starts. I suggested that we have someone on site that can actually do the job. Would you be up for it? I know you've got a few personal issues, so say no if you want but it would be great if you could. Let me know and I'll make arrangements.

LOL Tams xx

Bella didn't need to think about it, she replied straight back.

Hi Tamsin,

Clapham or Miami in January, tough choice but Miami wins. Not even the grief your artists give me could be worse than the grief I get outside of work, so go for it.

Best regards,
B

Bella knew it would be really hard work but it at least it would get her away from all the stuff at home. She was already dreading this week as it was Jen's monthly supper and the smug baby on boards, aka Susannah and Andrew, were due round on Friday and surprise, surprise, Alex managed to secure an invite. Jen repeatedly assured Bella that Susannah and Andrew had a list of no go topics including Alex's job, Alex's drinking, the fact Bella had left Alex, failed IVF, pregnancy and marriage.

Bella secretly agreed with Guy that they would keep a score of how many times Andrew and Susannah mentioned one of the taboo subjects. Bella had a fiver on 15 times and Guy had put a fiver on 10.

Friday night was the smug 'baby on boards' night featuring Barren Bella and Alcoholic Alex. It was going to be the first time Bella had seen Alex since her grand exit and she wanted to look like she was coping. Bella decided to have her hair done and buy a new top. Her stomach was still bloated after the IVF but her top held it all in. Thank God for Lycra.

Bella got home from work early to find a note from Jen. She had prepared the supper but was out at a music and movement class and wouldn't be back until 7 p.m. Bella decided to have a mammoth getting ready session. Sod it, she had nothing else to do. Two hours to get ready, she'd show them that Barren Bella could do glamour at least.

The Lycra top worked until she sat down, then the fat seemed to roll over the top of her hipsters and into Lycra rolls that hung like a stack of tyres around her stomach.

Jen returned with the children who had been given tambourines as a Christmas gift from the music clown. Jen looked exhausted.

"How was music and movement?"

"Bit too much movement from my two, and I nearly threw those bloody tambourines out the window onto the A23. How are you feeling about seeing Alex? You look fab by the way."

"Thanks, bit nervous to be honest. I think if it was just the four of us it would be okay, but Andrew and Susannah make me anxious. I didn't want it cancelled on my part. It's the last get-together before Christmas. Do you want me to feed and bath the kids while you get ready?"

"That would be great. I thought I would make an effort it's nearly Christmas and Guy is always complaining that I live in jogging bottoms."

"Okay, I'll take control while you go and glam up."

Bella fed Jake and Maddie and was busy playing orchestras when Guy appeared, late as usual.

"Hi kids, wow look at those tambourines. Daddy could hear those outside. They're amazing. Bloody hell Bells, you look amazing."

Bella felt herself blush, she didn't know why.

"Thought I'd make a bit of an effort, you know, in the festive season."

"Alex best watch out you know, with you walking around like that, you're a bit of a man magnet."

"I think he's fairly safe Guy, I don't really get out much. In fact, I spend most of my time indoors here."

"Exactly."

Bella decided not to continue the conversation and busied herself with tidying up toys and laying the table for Jen.

Guy decided to bath Jake and Maddie, and Bella put her feet up with a gin and tonic. She was starting to feel nervous.

Jen eventually appeared with Jake and Maddie who wanted one more recital of Jingle Bells with Aunty Bells before bedtime. Jen managed to squeeze into a black dress and put her make up on. Bella thought she looked gorgeous. She always had such a natural radiant beauty to her that no amount of make up and potions could ever create.

"Looking good girl."

"Guy just told me not to go outside in my black dress as I might cause a lunar eclipse, cheeky bastard."

"Ignore him, men really have no idea."

In the middle of the final recital, Alex arrived.

Bella couldn't believe it but she was actually shaking, or failing that the tambourine had taken on a life of its own. He looked awful. Mind you it was fair to say that Alex could do tragic if required, she blamed his mother.

"Great music kids, please don't stop on my account. I didn't realise you were so musical Bella. Carry on, I'll go and find Guy."

Jen immediately grabbed Bella.

"He looks awful Bella, did you see his face when he saw you and the kids? He's in the kitchen. Go and talk to him. Guy is still in the shower."

"Okay."

Alex sat at the kitchen table with a glass of water.

"You don't need to sit on your own Alex."

"You look great Bella and really happy with the kids. I've screwed up big time, haven't I?"

"I'm not blaming you Alex."

"I miss you so much. I have a job interview on Monday."

"That's great news!"

"It's been really difficult. Christmas isn't a good time of year to get work you know."

"Let me think…. big stomach, red nose…. have you tried the local Grotto?"

"Very funny. I bumped into an old mate from school. He's been out of work for six months. I'm worried if it takes too long, I'll lose you."

"Look, Alex, us getting back together isn't dependent on you getting a job so long as you're sober and going for interviews as opposed to pints. I can live with that."

"I haven't had a drink since you left you know. I've also been given these life-coaching books. I'm normally not into that sort of thing but I've been so down that they have been quite helpful and I promised Samantha I'd give them a shot."

"Samantha?"

"Yeah, one of the assistants from the trading desk. She only lives a couple of streets away and she heard about what happened at work and popped round. Quite nice really as none of the other bastards has been in touch."

Bella was just going to ask how old she was when Andrew and Susannah arrived. Susannah was wearing a maternity poncho and looked like she had swallowed an orange, she was still so bloody skinny.

"Hello you two. Bloody hell, you look like you're in a session at Relate. Mind you, I suppose you have to do that these days. Good God, Alex, you look awful. You can tell he hasn't got you chained to the kitchen sink any more Bella."

God she hated Andrew sometimes.

Guy started sorting the drinks out.

"Darling, Andrew and I were so sorry to hear about the IVF failure and your marriage breakdown."

Bella discreetly flicked two fingers at Guy. It looked like she was going to win the bet. Guy was trying not to laugh.

"So Alex old chap, I bumped into Dominic in Traders the other day. He was really cut up about having to let you go. Times are tough out there and only the very best make it these days. Anyway when I told him about the IVF, he felt awful. I said you losing your job had tipped you both over the edge and, well, who knows why these things fail. Mind you, as I said to him, the drinking won't have helped. I told him not to feel too bad. I reminded him of one of the City rules. You have to put personal lives aside. Businesses only run on results and tough decisions have to be made."

Bella flicked two more fingers at Guy, who was waving a white napkin above his head much to everyone's confusion.

Bella couldn't help but feel sorry for Alex. She could imagine the talk on the trading desk.

Alex looked like he was going to explode.

"Thanks Andrew. Just when I'm trying to get work in the City to get back with Bella you tell my old boss who will in turn tell the trading desk who will then tell anyone in the City who doesn't already know that I don't get results of any description including getting my wife pregnant and that I'm an alcoholic."

"Don't be so sensitive Alex, I'm sure you'll get work. There's always work if you look hard enough."

"Yeah, sure, I saw an advert for new staff in Blockbusters when I rented a DVD. It might be my only option after your contribution to my efforts. Let's hope you don't lose your job and Susannah doesn't leave you because I don't think your parents could fit you and your great big ego in their two-bedroom terrace. Whoops, sorry Susannah, I forgot. You thought they had a country house near Michael and Catherine."

"What do you mean, they only have two bedrooms? I thought we were going there for New Year. You know I want to do Wales." "Ignore him Susannah. Alex has always been jealous of our lifestyle."

"Hardly, money can't buy everything you know, including the complete lack of respect you have for your parents and your upbringing. You won't even introduce Susannah to your own family. What happens when they want to meet their grandchild? You need to take a long hard look at yourself Andrew. Stop kidding Susannah that you come from a wealthy background. There's nothing wrong with coming from a council estate in Cardiff, so just get on with it."

"My God darling is that like a trailer park?"

"We'll talk about this later. If you want to play games with me, Alex, I'll make sure you never work in the City again."

"Good, because to be honest I'm sick of being around tossers like you."

Alex grabbed his coat and stormed out of the kitchen. Bella was stunned. She knew this had been brewing for years but couldn't believe even Andrew would kick Alex when he was down.

"I'm going after him."

"Leave it Bella, why can't you just see you're married to a loser. Even you with your unbelievable tolerance levels must recognise that he's let you down and let himself down. He couldn't even get through a cycle of IVF sober." Clearly couldn't get you pregnant with brewer's droop and so you did IVF and hello, the machinery still isn't functioning."

"That's enough Andrew, we don't know why our IVF failed and so don't sit there with your smug wife stroking her pregnant stomach and tell me it failed because of Alex's drinking."

Bella rushed out to catch up with Alex. He was trying to hail a cab, but it was pouring with rain and they were all taken.

"Alex, wait."

"Look I'm sorry Bella. I couldn't take any more of that."

"Don't worry. He's a tosser. I'd love to be a fly on the wall when Susannah starts the trailer park inquisition later. I bet she won't want to spend New Year in Wales now."

"Do you think I went too far?"

"Not nearly as far as he did, don't worry about them. Oh look, there's Susannah's Mercedes. They've just left. I bet she couldn't delay her inquisition any further."

"Shall we go back to Jen's? She cooked a nice dinner and you look like you haven't eaten well recently."

"I've had takeouts and stuff. I think cutting back on beer has made me lose some weight and, of course, all the worry."

Bella and Alex raced back in the rain and were greeted by a round of applause from Guy.

"Well done mate. About time something was said. Susannah was bright red when she left. Same colour as that rug with a hole in it she was wearing."

Jen appeared out of the kitchen "It's called a poncho darling, I was thinking of getting one for Christmas."

"Don't waste your money Jen. I've got an old car rug that will just fit you fine. I'll get the kitchen scissors out and cut a whole in the middle. We'll save a fortune."

Jen ignored the comment.

"Come in you two, there's more supper to go around now. You're both soaking wet."

The rest of the evening was fairly uneventful. Alex tried to talk Bella into going home with him but Bella wasn't going to budge. She needed to be sure Alex was going to change for life and not just for Christmas. She was still wondering who the bloody hell Samantha was...

Chapter 25
Snogs, Lies and Space Hoppers

It was Christmas Eve and the office was nearly empty. Bella had volunteered to work because she wanted to keep busy. Anthony called her to say she could leave at 4 p.m., Happy Christmas.

Bella agreed with Alex that he could come round on Christmas Day with Ginger, and Jen made up another spare bed so they could stay. On Boxing Day, Bella was going to see her parents and Alex was going to see his mother. Ginger was staying with Jen and Guy, much to their children's delight.

Bella had spoken to Alex every day and he was starting to sound more positive. Bella secretly hoped he would have sorted himself by Christmas. She wanted to go back to him and was becoming paranoid that Samantha would be younger, thinner and fertile.

Having spent Anthony's Christmas bonus on a haircut and facial, Bella was starting to get into the festive spirit. She was looking forward to seeing Jake and Maddie on Christmas morning. She had bought them loads of stuff. It wasn't like she had kids of her own to spoil.

Jen was next door with the children when Bella arrived back from work and Guy was busily wrapping their presents.

"Hi Bella, I've been dying for you to get home. I desperately need help with wrapping this stuff. I have to get it done before Jen gets back. How the hell do you wrap a space hopper?"

"No idea."

"I tell you what, let's have a bottle of wine and think about it."

"Great idea."

Between them they managed to drink a bottle of wine and wrap thirty presents in under an hour, until they got to the space hopper.

"Right, we need another bottle to tackle this son of a bitch."

"Is it me Guy or is that space thing giving me funny looks?"

"No, you're right, it's evil. I cannot believe Maddie wants one of these."

Bella was starting to feel light-headed. Wine without any food was never a good plan.

"Right, I'm going in."

Guy grabbed the space hopper and they both started wrestling with the wrapping paper and the hopper.

Bella could not stop laughing. It was hopeless.

"Let's admit it Guy, even Santa would sack us. We're terrible at this. Neither one of us would make it into Santa's team of helpers. Although I do think your elf-like ears might help your case."

"I really like you Bella."

"Love you too, elf friend."

"I'm serious, since you've been living here I've realised how stupid Alex has been letting you leave. You make me laugh. We laugh together. Jen and I have lost that. She's completely immersed in the children. She hasn't time for me any more and I cannot do anything right where the kids are concerned."

"Life is bound to change when you have children. You need to talk to Jen and tell her how you feel. You're blessed with two beautiful children and have a third on the way. You owe it to them to let Jen know how you feel. She probably isn't even aware."

Guy was staring at her in a strange way.

"Guy, are you okay?"

"I don't know how to say this."

"Say what?"

"I've fallen for you big time. It's always been there Bella, right from when Alex introduced us all those years ago. We've always laughed at the same things and since you've been living here, I can't stop thinking about you. God, this is embarrassing, you don't feel the same way do you?"

Bella was lost for words. Where had this all come from? Guy made the odd comment over the years and Alex always said to Bella that he thought Guy flirted with her, but Guy flirted with everyone. Great, on Christmas Eve one of her husband's best friends was making a play for her and not only that, his wife had offered to donate her bloody eggs.

"It's the wine talking Guy, just get on with the space hopper."

Guy grabbed both of her hands and looked into her eyes.

"It's not the wine Bella."

Before Bella could reply, Guy was kissing her. Bella felt herself responding.

Suddenly the lounge door flung open.

"Mummy, mummy, Daddy's kissing Aunty Bella under the Christmas tree."

Guy immediately sprang backwards and threw himself on top of the space hopper.

169

"Daddy, what are you doing?"

A rather flustered Jen appeared at the door.

"Maddie, go and help Jake undo his coat."

"But mummy"

"Now!"

Bella started to feel sick. How were they going to explain this? She didn't want Guy; she loved Alex.

Jen flopped on the sofa.

"Guy, I'm so sorry. I meant to call you before we got back so you'd have time to finish wrapping the presents, did she see the space hopper?"

Bella was starting to panic. Had Jen heard Maddie's comment about the kissing?

"Not sure. I tried to throw myself on it but Bella and I have been up against it Jen. Trying to wrap this space hopper is a nightmare. What's all this about kissing? Is she starting to make up stories Jen? Is that what they teach them at Mother & Toddler group? Quite frankly it's not what I would expect from a three year old."

Bella could not believe Guy's front.

"I know, she makes up stories about Jake all the time. Says he's taken one of her toys when he hasn't. Probably just a phase."

"Well, I'm not happy about it Jen. Do you want me to get them ready for bed whilst you wrap the space hopper with Bella? If I try and wrap that thing one more time it'll take more than a puncture repair kit to sort it out. Right, I'll leave you to it."

"Bella I'm so sorry, leaving you with the miserable sod of Christmas past to wrap the kid's presents. I didn't realise how long it would take."

"Oh don't worry, we're nearly there."

Bella couldn't quite believe she was having a normal conversation with Jen two minutes after snogging her husband. She still felt flustered.

"Have you heard from Alex?"

"Yes, he'll be here with Ginger at 11 a.m. I've bought him a few presents. I'm really going to miss him when I wake up in the morning. It's always really nice on Christmas morning with just the two of us."

"Guy said he's doing really well. He's stopped drinking and lost loads of weight."

"He does seem to be making an effort. I hope it's for my benefit and not someone else's."

"What do you mean?"

"He's mentioned a girl a few times who he used to work with, Samantha. She's been giving him life coaching or something."

"If he'd shagged her, he'd tell Guy and he hasn't mentioned anything so I guess there's nothing in it."

"Do you think men and women can ever just be good mates or if they get on, is there always an undercurrent that could lead to something else?"

"Of course you can have mates of the opposite sex. Look at you and Guy, you've always got on well but it's just a friendship."

"You're right, I just don't want to lose Alex that's all."

"You won't."

Guy was shouting for Jen. Maddie was refusing to get ready for bed. Jen calmly dealt with the children and laid out carrots for the reindeers and single malt for Santa Guy.

Bella decided to have an early night. She could not face Guy alone again after their Christmas snog. She hoped he didn't think there was more to it. It was the last thing she needed right now. This was turning into the Christmas from hell. Roll on Miami. Tamsin called and her flight was booked for the 6th of January. She was only going to be away for three nights and Tamsin warned her that she would be

Rachel Watson

on tantrum management. How could it possibly be any more stressful than avoiding the advances of her best friend's husband and listening to Alex moan about her absence?

Chapter 26
Drugs and Diamonds

Christmas morning was chaotic. The children were completely overwhelmed by the experience and present opening had commenced at 6 a.m. Maddie threw up twice over her space hopper and Jake seemed to be more interested in opening presents that did not belong to him.

Bella bought a new outfit for Christmas Day and took extra time getting ready. The Christmas Eve snog with Guy made her sure of one thing - she still loved Alex. The only thing stopping her going back to him was the fear he'd let her down again.

Jen looked knackered. They agreed that Bella and Jen would cook the lunch whilst Guy tried to control the children. Bella spent most of the morning avoiding Guy. Fortunately, Maddie hadn't mentioned the kissing word again and Bella hoped the whole issue was forgotten. There was a chance they may need Jen's eggs, but not Guy's bloody sperm as well.

At the stroke of 11 a.m., Alex appeared with Ginger. Maddie and Jake immediately removed Ginger from his cage and introduced him to the Christmas tree. Clearly Alex hadn't bothered with a tree as Ginger seemed quite excited by the whole experience.

Bella noticed that Alex left a huge box in the hall with a large bow. She wondered if he had boxed up her possessions to make room for Samantha. God, she was starting to get paranoid.

Guy and Jen deliberately left them in the sitting room while they laid the table.

Bella decided to make the first move.

"Do I get a Christmas kiss then?"

"Well I wasn't sure if it was allowed what with us being er…"

"Estranged?"

"That's right, I guess I'm just confused about the boundaries, that's all."

"Well, it is Christmas."

Alex pulled her close.

"I've missed you so much. Am I still in the doghouse? I've done loads you know. I've had this life coaching stuff and well, I've made a few decisions."

"Life coaching? Is that the stuff you're doing with Samantha then?"

"Yeah, it's really good."

"How often do you do it then? The life coaching I mean."

"Well, it's an ongoing programme."

"So do you go to classes, or is it one on one?"

"Samantha pops round a couple of times a week. She's doing a course on it and I'm her experiment."

"Really Alex, what's the experiment? How quickly she can get her feet under the table and into the marital bed while your wife's away?"

"Oh my God, Bella, you don't think that something's going on do you? She's got a heart of gold, but she's as ugly as sin. If you saw her Bella believe me you wouldn't think anything was going on. I'm helping her with her course and she's helping me with my life."

"So what's changed then?"

"Lots actually. I've got some news. I wanted to wait until Christmas to tell you."

"Go on."

"Well, now I have my life goals."

"Cut the crap Alex, what's changed?"

"Okay, I've quit drinking, started undergoing acupuncture to improve my sperm count and, wait for it, got a job."

"That's fantastic, Alex. Obviously Samantha's programme is working better than my nagging."

"Not at all, you were right. We both needed space to sort our lives out and I feel like I'm really on track. I must have put you through hell Bella, and I'm so sorry."

Bella felt the tears start to run down her face. He had been really trying. She just hoped she was part of his new life goals.

"So what's the news on the job front then?"

"I had to take a long hard look at my life and I've come to the conclusion that the City's not good for me nor for us. I love the cut and thrust of the trading desk but hate the backbiting politics and people trying to be something they're not, just look at Andrew. You can't have personal problems on the trading desk. It's all about results, not people. I couldn't cope with trying to keep my job and making all the necessary IVF appointments. As you know, the IVF timescales are non-negotiable and my absence from the desk meant that we screwed up a big deal."

"Are you telling me this process cost you your job?

"Well, my days were numbered anyway, but it certainly didn't help."

"So what are you going to do now, start a landscaping garden business or become a vet? I have noticed you have been bonding with Ginger a lot of late."

"Well, I talked to my brother. You know I've resisted going into the family business for years. It so happens he's looking to buy some businesses across Europe and needs my expertise in negotiating the best deals. I didn't realise but his business is going really well and although we don't always get on, we've agreed to bury the hatchet and, well, I start work next week. Mother is over the moon, and as you know it's what Dad always wanted, both sons in the family business. I think it'll be great. At least I won't be answerable to the likes of Dominic any more. Maybe I have too much respect for people and can't hack the City. The one thing I remember about my father was his unquestionable respect for people and this new opportunity with my brother could be great, not only for our future but also fulfilling what my father always wanted."

"Are you sure it's what you want?"

"I'm sure."

"Well in that case, that's fantastic news Alex. I'm thrilled for you."

"Be thrilled for both of us Bella, I'm not just doing this just for me you know."

"Did you say something about acupuncture?"

"Yeah, I found this guy in Harley Street who put me on a programme to improve my sperm count and I've been having acupuncture to reduce my stress."

"How's it going?"

"Really well, and it's helped me to stop drinking. I feel fantastic. I know it's early days but I'm totally committed to doing this. I know I've let you down with the whole IVF thing Bella and I realise now that I may have jeopardised our chances of having a family but I am back on track. Bella please can we give it another go?"

"I didn't realise you'd done so much to try and sort things out. I'm proud of you and I never stopped loving you, you must know that."

"Well, I wasn't sure."

"I was always sure. You have put me to shame. I'm still obsessing over having a baby and painting my nails in bed. Do you think I need a life coach?"

"No, I want you back Bella. I wouldn't ask you to change a thing."

Bella was choking back tears. Alex pulled her close and they were suddenly kissing passionately. It was like when they first met.

"Mummy mummy, Uncle Alex is kissing Aunty Bella like Daddy did last night."

Bella and Alex sprang apart.

Alex looked surprised.

Jen rushed in from the kitchen.

"Sorry, Maddie has started to tell stories haven't you, Maddie? Why don't you help mummy find the Christmas crackers and leave Aunty Bella and Uncle Alex alone."

"But mummy…."

"Now."

"What the hell was that about Bella?"

"It's a long story, involving a space hopper. Do you really want to know?"

"I guess not. Anyway I've brought you a present. Hang on a second. "

Alex returned with the box he left in the hall.

"Go on, open it."

"Bloody hell Alex, I feel bad. I've only got you a few bits."

"Don't worry, just open it."

Bella ripped off the paper and found a plain white box. She quickly ripped it open.

"Syringes, drugs, these are IVF syringes Alex."

"I realise it might seem a strange gift but I really want us to give it another go. Oh, and there is another box inside it."

Bella pulled out the smaller box.

"What's this, drugs in miniature?"

"Just open it."

Bella opened the small box to find the most exquisite pair of diamond earrings.

"My God Alex, they're gorgeous, they must have cost a fortune."

"Not as much as the drugs, believe me. So can we have another go?"

"Of course."

"Are you coming back with me and Ginger tonight?"

"Yes. I can't believe this, it's the best Christmas present ever."

"What, the diamond earrings or the concoction of drugs containing, what was it? Menopausal hamster's wee."

"Both, I love them both."

"Mummy, Uncle Alex bought Aunty Bella a hamster for Christmas and it's wee weed in the box." Maddie had been hiding behind the Christmas tree.

Guy put his head round the corner.

"Honestly, Maddie, will you stop telling stories."

Alex laughed.

"Well, she's nearly right."

"Oh good Lord, please don't tell me you've bought Bella a rodent for Christmas."

"No, just IVF drugs. We're giving it another go, and we're back together. Well, at least I think we are?"

"Yes, we are."

Guy looked visibly shaken. "Is this what you really want Bella?"

"Totally."

"I guess this calls for a celebration, bring on the champagne Jen, they're back together. Do you need her eggs or what?"

Alex was quick to reply.

"We're going to have one more go with Bella's and then we'll see but we're still really grateful for the offer."

Jen hugged both of them.

"This is wonderful news you two. You're miserable sods apart so please don't let it come to this again, will you?"

"No," they said in unison.

"So when do you start shooting up again Bella?"

Before Bella could reply Alex butted in.

"As soon as, sod the blood tests, we're going for it."

Jen looked confused. "Will that work across time zones?"

Bella just remembered she hadn't told Alex about Miami.

"Sorry, Alex, I forgot to mention. I'm going to Miami with work in a week's time, but I'm sure it'll be fine. I'm going with Tamsin and she travelled through all her cycles of IVF and as for the other clients, they're all very familiar with syringes. We can check with the Doctor, but I'm sure it'll be fine."

"But you always rely on me to inject you."

"I'm only away for three nights. I can either do them myself or Tamsin can help. Don't worry, it'll be fine."

Jen reached for an envelope.

"We are so happy for you both, I bought you this for Christmas ages ago Bella. I wasn't going to give it you until later, but it's kind of relevant now."

Bella tore open the envelope.

"Four sessions with a hypnotist?"

Guy snatched the envelope from Bella.

"Jen have you gone mad? Is this to help Bella escape the reality of her failed IVF cycle by turning into a cat or something?"

"It's not stage hypnotism Guy, it's with a clinical hypnotist. He was on the television, and he specialises in infertility. He claims that many women experiencing infertility believe they can't get pregnant, something to do with the subconscious mind working against them, so they don't get pregnant. He re-programmes your thinking so you believe you can get pregnant and your mind accepts it as a possibility. He's helped several women get pregnant."

"Yeah right, probably shagged them whilst they were under his spell."

"Oh shut up Guy, I just thought it might help, that's all."

"It's a wonderful gift Jen, really thoughtful. It's certainly worth a try."

They all enjoyed the rest of the day. Ginger managed to find the turkey carcass and was sick under the Christmas tree but apart from that it was a very pleasant day.

Bella and Alex left before the children went to bed. They really wanted to spend Christmas night together. Bella hoped Alex hadn't noticed the tears in Guy's eyes as he helped load Bella's case into the car.

Chapter 27
Drugs and Rock n' Roll

Tamsin was an absolute star. She made all the arrangements for Bella to take the syringes on the flight and even arranged an upgrade for her.

Anthony was miffed when he heard he was banned from the Miami trip and when he found out Bella was travelling in Business Class with Tamsin he completely lost it. He made it known that staff should know their place and only travel down the back. Tamsin fired off one of her exocet emails and Anthony was suddenly taken ill with flu.

Things were going really well with Alex, and Bella started her hypnotherapy course. Curiously, she had the first dream in her life where she was pregnant. Jen was delighted, Guy took the piss and Alex remained neutral.

They decided not to have any blood tests and just go ahead with the cycle. Bella was nervous about the trip to Miami. She tried to inject herself but couldn't so Tamsin kindly offered help. Bella still couldn't quite get her head around Tamsin, the client from hell, injecting her at 32,000 feet en-route to Miami. Mind you, it couldn't be worse than Alex after ten pints of lager!

Alex made no secret of the fact that he was worried about Bella travelling to Miami. They had cleared it with the Doctor and been assured that so long as she managed the injections around the time differences, it wouldn't be a problem. She arranged to meet Alex at Heathrow on her return and they were going to go straight for a scan. Alex even bought her a world clock so she could time the injections.

The flight was full of clients on their way to the music awards. Bella watched in horror as the sixth bottle of champagne rolled down the aisle. The flight was packed and very bumpy. It had been 'fasten seat belts' most of the way. Bella was drinking water but noticed that Tamsin was knocking back champagne. Alex would be panicking if he could see this. Tamsin had another few hours of champagne drinking before it was injection time.

Bella decided to get some sleep. Although she was working, she promised Alex that she would try and take it easy.

"Bella, wake up, it's time."

A rather flushed Tamsin was prodding her. Apparently she'd set her travel alarm so they didn't miss the time. A number of passengers were looking rather concerned.

"It's a bloody alarm clock," Tamsin announced to the cabin.

The seat belt signs were still on and the aircraft was bouncing all over the place.

"What the hell are we going to do Tamsin? The seat belt signs are on and the trolley girls won't let us go to the loo."

"Panic not, I have a plan."

"Honestly Tamsin, we can't do it in the toilets."

"No, but we do have a couple of large blankets. You go under one and pull your trousers down and I'll prepare the syringe under the other one. We'll then pull the blankets together into a sort of tent effect and I'll jab you."

"I don't think it's going to work."

"It will. Anyway our lot are all too pissed to notice."

Tamsin disappeared under the blanket and nudged her when she was ready. Bella pulled the blanket over her head and undid her trousers.

"Oh my God darling, how fab is this? It's like being in the Girl Guides."

"I don't think administering drugs in severe turbulence at 32,000 feet would earn you a proficiency badge for your Girl Guide uniform, do you?"

"No idea. I got chucked out after two weeks for snogging a scout."

"Can you just get on with it?"

"I'm trying, believe me. Does this pilot know what he's doing? Surely it can't be this bumpy. Can't he just go higher or something, do you want me to ask him?"

"Just get on with it."

"I'm worried I'll miss."

"Don't be, I've got spares."

Tamsin went for it. The needle went in just as the aircraft lurched forward.

"Aarrrggghhh" screamed Bella.

Suddenly the tent was no more.

Oh my God, it was the record label's latest signing, this gorgeous Irish guy who won one of the talent shows on TV.

"Wow excellent! I knew this business would be cool. Two lesbians under a blanket getting it on and doing drugs. Fantastic!"

Before Bella could respond, Tamsin took control.

"Piss off will you, and if you want to be looked after in Miami you'll keep this quiet do you understand? I've been in this business longer than you've been alive, so be a good lad and get back to your seat. "

"Oh my God Tamsin I don't believe this."

"Ignore him. He's too pissed to remember. Did it all go in?"

"Definitely."

"Thanks Tamsin. Let's hope the return flight isn't quite so bumpy."

"If that little wannabe catches us under the blankets again, we could be in trouble."

Bella laughed. She couldn't wait to tell Alex.

The next few days in Miami were really hectic. As expected all the artists were totally unreasonable. It was worse than looking after Jake and Maddie. Alex was texting her relentlessly to see if she was okay and Tamsin was fussing over her, much to the delight of their new signing. She was convinced he thought he might see some more lesbian action before the trip was over.

Bella went to bed around 2 a.m. every morning and fell asleep to the tape her hypnotist prepared for her. She drifted off with images of a garden with a swing with herself, Alex and their baby playing on the grass. Occasionally one of the cokehead pop stars would pop up on the swing, but she always managed to get rid of them with a machine gun. God, this hypnotherapy stuff was good!

Bella couldn't wait to get home and see Alex. She was anxious about the scan but was trying to remain positive. The return flight was a lot calmer and Bella managed to shoot up in the toilets with Tasmin when everyone was sleeping. All of the clients were partied out. It had been a really good awards show for them. Only two hotel suites had been trashed and only two members of the press had been punched. It had been hugely successful really, by the standards of previous shows.

Bella was knackered when she arrived at Heathrow. She guessed the combination of the drugs and jet lag wouldn't be too great. Alex was at arrivals with two bunches of flowers -

one for her and one for Tamsin. Tamsin was clearly delighted and couldn't stop hugging both of them.

The Irish wannabe was staring at all of them.

"Man, you lot are weird."

"What's he going on about?"

Tamsin laughed, "Don't worry Alex, he caught us under our blankets, me with a syringe and Bella with her trousers down. He thinks we're a pair of lesbian druggies."

"Oh my God."

"Don't worry, it's quite normal in our business. Good luck with the scan. Text me when you know."

Alex and Bella raced to the hospital. Bella hoped the time difference hadn't affected the treatment.

There were eight follicles. She had responded well to the treatment again. It was fantastic news.

Bella agreed with Anthony that she wouldn't go back to work after the flight so she spent the rest of the day drifting in and out of sleep listening to her hypnotherapy tape and dreaming of babies, rock stars and machine guns. Surely it had to work this time.

Chapter 28
Mr Fresh and Mr Frosty

It was egg retrieval day. Bella and Alex were nervously waiting for the consultant to give them the results.

"Why is he taking so long to get round Alex, we were first on?"

"They're really busy, don't panic."

"It bloody hurts this time."

"In what way?"

"Really bad stomach cramps, I think it's normal. I guess I was just lucky last time."

Bella was listening to the couple in the bed next to them. Lucky cow had fifteen superb eggs apparently. Bella was starting to feel edgy. She had gone down to theatre before them.

"Grab the doctor Alex, I really can't wait any longer."

Alex dashed after him and he promised to return with their notes in a few minutes.

"Something is wrong Alex, I just know it."

"Don't panic, he's just busy. Look, he's here."

"Right Mr & Mrs Moore, as you know there were eight follicles, and we managed to retrieve two eggs as the rest were immature."

Was it Bella's imagination or had the rest of the ward gone silent? Great, so she was their worst egg performer today. Fabulous, she hoped that Alex wouldn't blame it on her trip to Miami.

Bella was the first to speak.

"That's not very good, is it? If we only have two, what if they don't fertilise?"

"They're of a decent quality and if they don't fertilise we've got the four you had frozen so hopefully you can still go ahead."

Even Alex looked fraught.

"What do you mean hopefully?"

"It's dependent on these eggs fertilising and if they don't and we go to the frozen ones, it's dependent on those embryos surviving the thawing process. We'll give you a call by midday tomorrow, please try and relax. It only takes one good egg. "

Bella waited until he left before saying anything.

"It only takes one good egg. What a bloody joke. We had two good eggs last time and it didn't work."

"Don't get so upset Bella please try and relax darling, my sperm's improved and like he said we only need one good egg."

They had a restless night. Bella was in pain and Alex was worried about her. She texted Tamsin who tried to reassure her that at least one would fertilise as they had fertilised before.

Alex took the call from the clinic. It wasn't great news. Only one had fertilised and they wanted to know if they would like to have the others defrosted.

Bella took the news badly. She was concerned that the quality of her eggs had worsened although both Alex and the clinic tried to reassure her that they hadn't. They decided to have the remaining four defrosted and spent another tense twenty-four hours wondering if they would survive the thawing process.

Eventually the clinic called, only one had made it. Bella was really worried. They had the transfer booked for the following day. One fresh embryo and one frozen, Mr Fresh and Mr Frosty as Alex called them.

Alex delayed starting his new job so he could go to the transfer with Bella. She didn't want to look at the embryos on the screen this time. It was too much seeing the grey blobs they created on the screen and knowing they could be lost again. She couldn't bear it.

The consultant was raving about the eight-cell size and quality of Mr Fresh. Bella could tell Alex was getting excited, especially when he realised there was a sunset at the time the catheter was inserted. Alex recalled the night they first started the baby making process in Bali. Bella didn't understand how he could possibly compare their spontaneous lovemaking during a sunset in Bali with an out-of-the-body conception experience during a sunset in Clapham. Bella preferred to remain neutral. She'd been there before and it was a bloody long way to fall.

Chapter 29
The P Word

Bella went back to work the day after the embryo transfer. She felt stressed. She had come down with a heavy cold and was scared to take anything just in case it affected Mr Fresh and Mr Frosty.

Anthony was being particularly difficult. Ever since she bonded with Tamsin, he was making her life miserable. She was struggling with twelve-hour days and didn't know what to do. On top of that, Alex and Tamsin were telling her to go to the doctors and get signed off. Bella agreed to meet Tamsin for a coffee. No doubt she was going to get another lecture.

"Bella, you look truly awful."

"I know, I feel it."

"Please go to the doctors, you can't go on like this."

"What am I going to say to him? I'm not ill. I'm stressed out with IVF and with work and I have a cold. He's hardly going to sign me off on that basis, is he? I've never asked for a sick note and besides, Anthony would go mad."

"I know, I've worked through IVF and it can be tough on you both emotionally and physically. On some cycles I was glad with the distraction; on others I felt quite ill and it was a chore. All I know is I nearly worked myself to death and they all failed. Don't do it, Bella. I'm begging you, if you don't feel well then go to the doctors. You've had three cycles virtually one right after the other and it's bound to take its toll. I want you to get signed off and if Anthony starts, I'll deal with him."

"Really?"

"Just do it."

Bella called Alex and told him she was going to try and get signed off. He reassured her that she looked terrible and if the doctor took one look at her, she'd be signed off. Safe in the knowledge that she looked terrible, Bella asked the doctor to sign her off until she was due a pregnancy test and, much to her delight, he agreed. For the first time ever she was going to lie in bed for two weeks with Ginger and eat chocolate. Fantastic!

Bella enjoyed her first few duvet days and then it started to drag. She couldn't believe daytime TV presenters could talk about the benefits of recycling dishcloths for a whole fifteen minutes. She hated being at home. Even the hypnotherapist's tape was starting to send her over the edge. Suddenly frozen babies were appearing with drunken rock stars and Ginger gave birth to a litter of kittens even though he was a neutered male. This wasn't good.

The only good thing was that Anthony had been very concerned since he received the doctor's note with stress and exhaustion cited as reasons for her absence. He probably thought she was going to sue him, so he sent flowers and chocolates.

Alex was fussing like crazy. He was determined to take on the household chores so Bella could rest. Bella did try and tell him that burning the dinner every night and tumble drying her cashmere sweater to the size that would probably fit Mr Fresh or Mr Frosty wouldn't increase their chances of success, but he was having none of it.

Bella stopped surfing the infertility chat rooms. There were numerous 'cycle buddies' as they called themselves. The whole thing made her more neurotic. Everyone seemed to be having different symptoms and the topic never varied. It was always the dreaded two-week wait. It was getting near her two weeks and some of her cycle buddies experienced some bleeding. Bella was having enough problems getting through her own IVF cycle let alone the cycles of thirty other buddies.

Jen called every day and asked if she wanted to go out. She was terrified someone from work might see her and politely declined every outing.

On day thirteen of the two-week wait, Bella finally lost it. She needed to get out as she was going mad. If she saw one more house or body makeover programme she would scream. So when Jen asked her if she wanted to go to the supermarket to help with Jake and Maddie, she leapt at the chance.

"Honestly Bella, I can't believe you're going to the supermarket with Jen and the kids. Even Guy refuses to go and he's their father. It's a nightmare apparently."

"It'll be fine. It can't be any worse than being stuck indoors with daytime TV."

Guy was right. The kids were a nightmare. Even Bella started to get annoyed when Maddie threw a temper tantrum by the fruit and veg because Jen wouldn't let her feed Jake raw chicken legs.

Bella wasn't feeling well which didn't help. She was hot and extremely irritated and what was that awful smell?

"Are you alright Bella, you don't look too good?"

"I guess after having two duvet weeks, this trip is proving more stressful than I thought."

"Sorry, the kids are being truly hideous. Guy's right, I should go online and have it delivered like you do."

"Yeah, it works really well for us. It's been ages since I've been in a supermarket. Have they always smelt so awful or is it the fact I haven't been in one for ages?"

"What do you mean smell awful?"

"That really strong bleach smell. It's making me feel sick, it's disgusting."

Jen dropped her bag of apples on the floor.

"I don't believe it - you're pregnant!"

"What are you talking about Jen? We won't know 'til tomorrow and I'm starting to have period cramps."

"You're pregnant, I'm telling you. I've always been exactly the same. The smell of bleach has me throwing up right from the first day I miss my period."

"Are you sure?"

"Positive, do you remember when I came to that infertility group with you and felt sick in the hospital corridor?"

"Yes, but honestly Jen I can't be, I've got period pains."

"I also had cramps with all three, not sure why."

"Honestly, Bella, you even *look* pregnant."

"How can I possibly look pregnant, I don't have a bump or anything?"

"Buy a pregnancy test. I can just tell from your face. I've always been able to tell early on."

"Who are you all of a sudden, Mystic Meg? I can't do it until tomorrow and I was going to wait for the blood test if I don't get my period. I can't face another missing blue line. I've been there too many times. I think I'm going to throw up, honestly Jen I feel really sick."

"Get used to it girl. I have the same sensation for the first fourteen weeks."

"Don't Jen, I just don't want to get too excited."

"Please just buy the test and go home, and call me tomorrow just to confirm."

"Confirm what?"

"The pregnancy stupid."

Bella decided to leave. The sickness was too much to handle. Maybe it was all in her mind. It could be the hypnotherapy tapes that were making her feel sick. She could be having one of those phantom pregnancies.

Bella got off the bus twice to be sick and her period cramps were getting worse. Maybe she was really ill after all.

Alex opened the front door. Bella bolted past him as she was going to be sick again. She just managed to make it to the bathroom. A beaming Alex greeted her.

"So?"

"So you're being sick, surely that means...."

"I've got period cramps."

"Oh."

"I think I might have a bug or something. I feel really rough. Jen is convinced I'm pregnant because I could smell bleach in the supermarket. I can't have a blood test until tomorrow."

"Could you do a pregnancy test today?"

"Yes, but we could get a false positive."

"Let's do it."

"I'm not sure if I can face it, Alex."

"You do what you need to do and leave it on the side. I'll check it."

Bella couldn't believe Alex talked her into doing a test. Part of her wanted to do the test just to stop the speculation. At least when it came back negative, she could prove to everyone that it was a bug and they would leave her alone.

Bella did the test and left it on the side. She sat on the bed with Ginger while Alex read the leaflet and waited for the result. Bella looked at her watch. At least sixty seconds had passed. What on earth was he doing? Finally, Alex emerged from the bathroom clutching the stick.

Alex sighed.

"Alex I told you I've got period pains. We've wasted so much money on these tests over the years, it's ridiculous."

"The test is positive."

"What? Are you sure?"

"Checked it three times, it's positive Bella, you're pregnant."

"Don't get too excited, Alex, I think we can get a false positive with IVF. We do need have to have a blood test done."

"But we've never had a positive test before. Surely with you being sick, you have to be pregnant."

"Before we frame the test and stock up on nappies, let me call the hospital and book in for a blood test tomorrow."

Neither of them slept that night. Bella kept being sick and Alex was edgy and excited. Bella knew they needed to see the outcome of the blood test before they began contemplating the idea that she could be pregnant.

Bella booked a 9 a.m. appointment and they were told they needed to wait one hour for the results. Bella couldn't talk about it, not even to Alex. She couldn't deal with the what ifs, only the facts.

She was avoiding texts and calls from Jen and felt safe in the hospital waiting room devoid of contact from the outside world. Even Alex was instructed not to speak so they sat in silence. Bella didn't take any notice of the distressed couples and the follicle production competition, which was kicking off behind well-thumbed copies of Hello. Feeling particularly hormonal and fraught, Bella would have loved to shout out at the top of her voice to the loudest competitor: "Think you're bloody clever do you producing 15 follicles, wait until 14 are immature or 13 don't fertilise and then come in here and talk about your sodding follicles? Wait until you have to come for a blood test to see if you are pregnant when your husband is eyeing up prams on the tube and you know you're not bloody pregnant. Welcome to the world of IVF, bitch."

My God, thought Bella, I'm seriously losing it. She nudged Alex.

"Sorry, can't speak, not allowed"

"Don't be difficult Alex"

"You told me…."

"I know what I told you. We've been waiting an hour and twenty-two minutes, what are they playing at?"

"Sorry?"

"I can't sit in here for one minute longer. Just tell the nurse I want my results now will you?"

"Mr and Mrs Moore, sorry to keep you waiting. All of the consultants are busy and we're trying to get you into see one of them. It could be another thirty minutes."

"So we've got to wait another thirty minutes to be told I'm not pregnant and be sold another cycle have we? Forget it."

"Bella, please calm down."

Bella had everyone's attention in the waiting room. Even the follicle producing competition came to a standstill. The nurse looked a little flustered.

"Mr and Mrs Moore, if you'd like to step outside."

"Why, to be told I need to wait to see a consultant? Forget it, we're leaving. I'm not prepared to do this any more, even with my best mate's eggs. Forget it, we're off."

Bella grabbed her coat and handbag.

"Mrs Moore, your test is positive."

"What does that mean exactly?"

"You're pregnant. We were waiting for a consultant to book you in for an early pregnancy scan to confirm everything is okay."

The fifteen follicle bitches were speechless.

Bella sat straight down. She was pregnant, the test was positive, and the words were ringing around her ears.

Luckily, Alex took control.

"Thank you for confirming that. We'll wait for the consultant."

The nurse looked relieved.

"I told you…."

"Not now Alex."

They sat in silence. It was only five minutes before a slot became available with their consultant.

"Congratulations, Mr and Mrs Moore."

Alex beamed, "Congratulations to you as well for making this possible."

Bella decided to take over.

"What's this about an early pregnancy scan? Don't you have one at twelve weeks and get a picture?"

"With IVF, Mrs Moore, we like to have a scan to check if everything has implanted in the correct position two weeks after the confirmation of pregnancy. We also look to establish if there is more than one."

"Of course, Bella, if both Mr Fresh and Mr Frosty made it we could be having twins."

"What are you saying, with IVF they don't always implant correctly, so I may not be pregnant?"

"Your test results confirm you are pregnant, and I don't anticipate any problems but I'd like to check. I've booked an appointment for you in two weeks' time."

Bella felt numb. For years she's been waiting to be pregnant, to say "I'm pregnant," to be able to produce scan photos and rub her stomach and now she felt nothing, absolutely nothing.

Alex was practically skipping up the street.

"Say something Bella, you're pregnant, not mute."

"We have to wait until we know everything's in the right place Alex. We need to wait for the scan."

"You heard the guy, he's sure everything's fine, can I tell my mother?"

"Nobody in their right mind tells people until they're at least twelve weeks. Because we know earlier than most due to the IVF doesn't mean we'll be telling anyone unless I make it to twelve weeks."

"What about Jen and Guy?"

"We'll tell them we are waiting for a scan to confirm, that's all."

"I thought this moment would be special Bella, celebratory almost. We've waited for this for years. Why are you so devoid of emotion?"

"I've no idea. It feels like I've got another hurdle to jump, the two-week scan. It's not like I'm sixteen, had a bag of crisps and a bottle of lager and suddenly got pregnant, is it? It's been a long painful process Alex, and I can't quite believe it or even want to believe it in case I wake up and it's not true."

"Sorry Bella, I never realised. It must be the shock after all this time."

"I'd rather not talk about it until we've had the scan, if that's okay?"

"Okay, try and keep calm. Chances are everything is fine but I understand you want to wait."

"No looking at three wheeler prams Alex, or having paternal chats with Guy please."

"I promise I won't mention the P word again until after the scan. Wow, did you see that?"

"What?"

"That pram, it was amazing, bit like a tripod. Mind you, not sure if you could fit twins into a tripod contraption."

"Alex, the P word covers pregnancy and prams, got it?"

"Sorry yes, got it."

Chapter 30
Another Scare

Bella felt strange going back to work after sick leave especially knowing she could be pregnant. Bella and Alex went to see Guy and Jen and explained that they wouldn't know for sure until the scan confirmed everything. Despite pleading with them not to discuss the fact she was pregnant, it seemed to be the main topic of conversation. She caught Alex on the Internet looking at prams at least five times and Jen seemed to think the fact she couldn't keep food down was the sign of a healthy pregnancy.

Bella strolled into Tamsin's office, the smell of Tamsin's rocket fuel coffee from her machine made Bella feel sick.

"Thank God you're back Bella. The temp they hired to cover you was useless, response times of a sloth and bloody rude. I complained to Anthony who told me he would personally look after all my bookings. Can you imagine? I told him I'd rather stick with the sloth. Anyway, how are things with you?"

"I'm pregnant."

Bella could hardly believe she was saying those words. In fact it was the first time she said the "P word" and "I'm" in the same sentence.

"Bella that's fantastic. I'm so pleased for you."

Tamsin was crying, still Bella felt nothing.

"I'm just waiting for the scan to confirm everything has implanted correctly and to determine how many are in there."

"How are you feeling?"

"Sick and numb is probably the best description. I'm constantly being sick, checking my knickers every ten minutes to see whether my period has come. I don't feel anything. I thought I'd be a gushing mother-to-be and rubbing my stomach but to be honest, I'm just waiting for the next thing to go wrong."

"A typical IVF pregnancy then."

"Really?"

"For sure, you talk to some of the girls at the support group who've had IVF babies. One girl would not believe she was pregnant until she had the baby safe in her arms, and then she was in bloody shock until the kid was a year old."

"That makes me feel better. I thought it was just me. Alex has gone into baby overdrive. He's on the Internet looking at prams and talking about upcoming sleepless nights with his mate. As for me, I don't even want to think about it, let alone talk about it until I'm certain. Any normal conception you can wait until you're at least three months. That way you can get your head round it, but with IVF the embryos have barely implanted and people are discussing christenings. I'm not going to tell my family until I'm three months pregnant, if I get that far."

"Of course you'll get that far. At least you're being sick. That's a good sign from what I've heard."

"According to Jen yes, apparently I should be grateful that I'm being sick, you know get at one with my vomit."

"Exactly. Promise me you'll tell me how it's going. Just think it will be payback time for all those bitches that have rubbed your nose in their vile grainy scan photos. I bet they won't have scan photos of their little so and so at a mere two weeks."

"I don't think we'll be able to see much."

"You can see sod all on most of them. It's only the parents who think they can tell who it looks like."

"When I get my two week photos, I'll bring them over for a coffee morning and we can agree who it or they look like."

"Could be twins?"

"Don't know. I just want everything to be okay."

"If you're having twins, can I be there when you tell Anthony?"

"I'll be selling ringside seats."

Bella returned to her desk. Sloth temp left her with a stack of work. She knew Anthony chose the temp with the cheapest rates to cover for her. Bella didn't know if it was the constant sickness or hormones but she was not in a great mood and to make matters worse, Anthony was due in to see her in ten minutes. Bella knew he would be checking to see if she was firing on all cylinders. She guessed he would not be happy, as Tamsin had been a handful while she was away.

Bella asked the receptionist to buzz her when Anthony was on his way to her office. The receptionist was always up for a game of Anthony Watch. Bella bought her a big box of chocolates every Christmas as a thank you. Bella could not face an Anthony ambush.

Bella's phone buzzed.

"He's in the building."

Bella felt sick again. She decided to throw up before he arrived in the office and managed to fit in a quick "vomit and go" in the ladies.

"Bella darling, how are you? Nice and relaxed after your sick leave?"

"Sorry?"

"I was concerned when I saw your doctor's note, Bella. Were you really stressed and exhausted?"

"No, Anthony, I thought I'd just have a couple of weeks off."

"Why, have you run out of holiday?"

Bella was starting to lose patience.

"I was off Anthony because I was stressed and exhausted and while you may think I've had a nice relaxing break, I can assure you I haven't."

"I hope you're not blaming work Bella because I've always supported you and if you think your job is stressful, well you should try mine. Tamsin was unbelievably difficult while you were off and that temp cost us a fortune."

"I am not blaming work, Anthony. I've just been through my third cycle of IVF and I've tried to juggle all of that with twelve hour days."

"Why didn't you tell me?"

"Because I wanted to carry on as normal, that's all, and I managed until this final treatment. I've honestly not felt well enough to work."

Anthony was finding the conversation difficult.

"Don't people normally have a few attempts at IVF?"

"Is this is your way of asking me if I am going to have more time off?"

"I need to plan that's all, Bella."

"Well, you better plan for cover for a year then because I'm pregnant. I'm just waiting for a scan to see if everything is okay and to check if I'm expecting twins. Oh, and while you're planning, don't cut corners by getting a cheap crappy temp in to cover me because Tamsin won't buy it."

"Are you officially telling me you're pregnant?"

"No, just helping you with your planning Anthony. Now if

you don't mind, I have lots of work to catch up on and I need to throw up before my next conference call."

"Will you need more time off for the scans and stuff?"

Bella's hormones were raging. She was struggling to breathe. She knew he had a business to run but after all her commitment through the years, she thought he could be a bit more supportive. Suddenly, Bella felt a cramp-like pain go through her stomach which took her by surprise. She gasped.

"Don't look so startled Bella, I'm only trying to plan that's all."

Bella bent over double with the pain. It felt like she was being stabbed. She pushed past Anthony and raced to the loo.

Fortunately, the loos were empty. She rushed into a cubicle and pulled her knickers down. She could hardly bear to look. Sure enough, in stark contrast to her white knickers was a bright red stain. Bella didn't know what to do. She grabbed her mobile out of her bag and called Tamsin.

"It's me, I'm in the ladies. What does a miscarriage look like?"

"Stay where you are, I'm on my way."

Bella sat on the floor waiting for Tamsin. She felt like a small child lost and confused.

Tamsin knocked on the cubicle door.

Bella quickly pulled up her knickers.

"Are you okay?"

"Not sure."

"What's happened?"

"I was having a row with Anthony and I started having pains so I raced here and…"

Bella could hardly get the words out. It felt like she was choking.

"…I found blood in my knickers, Tamsin."

"How much?"

"Not a lot."

"Okay, calm down. Some women bleed when they're pregnant. It's called implantation bleeding or something like that. It might be a good sign. Come back to my office and we'll call your IVF clinic, they'll know what to do."

Tamsin took over, telling Anthony to piss off when she bumped into him in the corridor. The IVF clinic didn't seem overly concerned and advised her to relax and wait for the two-week scan. Tamsin, however, insisted on taking her to the nearest doctor at the local centre where you could pay to see someone. They decided not to tell Alex until they knew everything was okay.

The doctor was really accommodating and saw them straight away, probably something to do with the amount of twenty-pound notes Tamsin was pulling out of her Gucci purse. The doctor came into the reception to find them.

"Bloody hell, he's good looking. Forget the NHS. I'm going to pay to see him in future. You're bound to feel better after 15 minutes with him, definitely worth the money."

Tamsin waited in reception while Bella saw the doctor.

"Please sit on the bed Mrs Moore, I'll be with you in a minute."

Bella took her trousers and knickers off; there was no more blood. Hopefully Tamsin was right, it wasn't a miscarriage.

The Doctor came in. Bella took a deep breath and opened her legs.

Bella couldn't understand why the doctor looked so surprised.

"Er, Mrs Moore, would you mind getting dressed please? I only want to take your blood pressure."

Bella thought she was going to die of embarrassment.

"I am so sorry. I have just had three cycles of IVF and well I'm er used to taking my knickers off for examinations and scans and stuff. I'm really sorry."

"Not to worry, just took me by surprise that's all."

Considering the rather difficult start the doctor was very calm and reassuring. It really was a waiting game. Nobody could do anything to prevent a miscarriage and after giving it some thought Bella decided the best option was to put the bleeding episode to the back of her mind and wait for the scan. The Doctor advised her to rest for a few days so she decided to call Anthony and tell him. Poor old Anthony had been worried sick. He thought he might have caused her to have a miscarriage. As a result, he was very amenable to Bella taking a few days off.

Bella just needed to get through the next couple of weeks, hopefully without any more scares. She desperately wanted to know everything was okay.

Chapter 31
Wheel Of Fortune

Bella and Alex were in Starbucks an hour before the scan.

"Move that bloody Mocha away from me Alex will you, it's making me feel sick"

"You've already been sick four times, surely there's nothing left."

"It doesn't work like that, just move the bloody Mocha."

"Are you nervous?"

"I'm terrified and last week's scare didn't help."

Alex finished his Mocha and Bella visited the loo twice more.

An hour later, Bella was in her normal IVF position, de-robed with legs splayed, waiting for the consultant.

"You're shaking Bella."

"I know that Alex, no need to draw attention to it."

The consultant came in and started setting up the machine.

"As you are aware Mr and Mrs Moore, it is still a vaginal scan at this point. We're looking to see if we can establish how many embryos have implanted and if they're in the correct place. Sometimes one of the little ones can hide and you think you've got one and then, we find two."

"Blimey how do you order a pram if you're not sure how many are going to go in it?"

Alex really was obsessed with prams; he had show Jen one on the internet. Jen laughed and told him he'd soon be out buying a cheap buggy that actually would fit in the car and erect without a support team of ten.

"Don't worry, we'll find out at the next scan for sure."

Bella felt very uncomfortable. She was on a small reclining bed and kept slipping on the large sheet of paper placed there in the name of hygiene. In addition to Alex bleating on about prams, the consultant was clearly struggling with the probe.

"Sorry Mrs Moore, this probe is not the best. I'm just going to try and guide it in."

Alex saw the consultant disappear between his wife's legs, for Bella's sake he managed to stop himself laughing. Bella was looking very uneasy.

"Mrs Moore, you really are a bit too far up the bed, could I just ask you to gently slide down the bed for me please."

Bella was about to oblige and gently pushed down when the paper sheet she was lying on seemed to take on a life of its own.

Alex looked on in horror as Bella slid down the bed and landed on the consultant's face.

Bella just wanted to die.

"Oh my God. I'm so sorry."

Bella was quickly trying to reverse off his face, she couldn't decide whether it was the probe or his glasses she could feel inside her.

Although the consultant was trying to remain calm, Bella could see him shaking as he wiped his glasses with a tissue. This was probably one of the most embarrassing moments of her life.

"Okay Mrs Moore, let's try again. Could you maybe hold onto something this time please?"

Bella grabbed Alex who was desperately trying to contain his laughter and failing miserably.

"Okay here we go."

Bella felt the probe go in. She was too shaken to think about what they might find.

"There you go. It's a single sac and it has implanted in a perfect position. Congratulations Mr & Mrs Moore, everything is fine."

Bella was unable to make the words that were forming in her brain move to her mouth.

"Great news doctor, is there definitely just one or could the other one be hiding?"

"I've got a really clear view and I'm pretty sure there's only one."

Alex looked at Bella.

"Do you think its Mr Fresh or Mr Frosty?"

Bella was opening her mouth like a goldfish and was still struggling to compute a sentence.

"I dunno Alex."

"I think it's likely Mr Moore that the fresh embryo will have survived and the frozen one will have failed to implant. Typically we have less success with frozen embryos, but there's no real way of knowing, it could be either."

Bella tried another sentence.

"I'm definitely pregnant then? I mean I did bleed, only once though. But I am pregnant aren't I? Do I need another test or scan?"

"We'll book you in for an eight week scan and we'll send your notes through to your GP who will arrange your twelve week scan. At this stage everything is fine and you are definitely pregnant. Do you have any more questions?"

"Can I have a print out of the scan please?"

"You can, but I'm afraid you can't really see a lot."

"It doesn't matter. I have a few people I need to show it to, that's all."

"Bella, I don't believe it. You're turning into one of those smug 'baby on boards' types who produces unidentifiable grey grainy scan pictures of aliens out of their handbag at a moment's notice."

"I know and guess what, I can't wait to get my alien pictures out!"

"Don't tell me we're going to have one of those 'baby on board' signs on the car."

"Absolutely, we made it against all the odds and I want everyone to know it."

"You're right, we played Baby Roulette and won. I'm so proud of you Bella."

"It takes two to make a baby in a petri dish Alex."

"I love you and Mr Fresh."

"I love you too and it could be Miss Fresh or Mr Frosty or even Miss Frosty."

"Either way it could be a great after dinner conversation for when Junior's older. Can you imagine, he can tell people he may have started life prior to conception, in a freezer? Bound to pull the chicks with that line."

"Before you start planning pick up lines, Alex, I still have the pregnancy to get through and I don't think we should count our chicken until he or she has hatched."

"Can I order the pram though, I really want one of those three-wheeler tripod ones?"

"Go for it, and see if they'll throw in a 'baby on board' sticker will you?"

"And a smug face?"

"No, I think we've already got two of those!"

Printed in the United Kingdom
by Lightning Source UK Ltd.
130425UK00001B/35/A